NEANDERTALS

NEANDERTALS
A PREHISTORIC PUZZLE

YVETTE LA PIERRE

 Twenty-First Century Books • Minneapolis

To Steve, Grace, and Camille

Twenty-First Century Books
A division of Lerner Publishing Group, Inc.
241 First Avenue North
Minneapolis, MN U.S.A. 55401

Website address: www.lernerbooks.com

Library of Congress Cataloging-in-Publication Data

La Pierre, Yvette Marie.
    Neandertals : a prehistoric puzzle / by Yvette La Pierre.
        p.   cm. — (Discovery!)
    Includes bibliographical references and index.
    ISBN 978–0–8225–7524–5 (lib. bdg. : alk. paper)
    1. Neanderthals—Juvenile literature. I. Title.
  GN285.L37 2008
  569.9'86—dc22   2007022066

Manufactured in the United States of America
1 2 3 4 5 6 – DP – 13 12 11 10 09 08

CONTENTS

On a sunny day in August 1856, workers were digging for lime-stone in a pretty valley near Dusseldorf, Germany. As they worked, their shovels hit some bones. The bones were embedded in a thick layer of mud in the cave they were working in, 60 feet (18 meters) above the valley floor. As the workers shoveled, a skull emerged. It had a low forehead with a heavy ridge above the eye sockets. As they continued to work their way farther into the cave, they unearthed more bones. Because most of the bones were thicker than those of a normal human, the workers thought they were probably those of an old bear. They tossed the bones down the slope into a pile of other junk from the cave. The boss, however, knew that the local schoolteacher was interested in natural history, so he put the bones aside for Johann Karl Fuhlrott.

Johann Fuhlrott liked to explore the hilly countryside, collecting specimens of wildflowers, bird's eggs, and the physical remains of ancient plants and animals, known as fossils. Like many educated Europeans in the nineteenth century, Fuhlrott was an amateur natural historian. He liked to study natural objects and organisms and their origins. Collecting plants and insects, exploring tidal pools, and sketching nature were popular pastimes for well-bred people. Exploring nature was considered a productive use of one's free time. It was also a good excuse for a young man and woman to go for a long walk together!

Workers found bones in the Neander Valley near Dusseldorf, Germany, in 1856 that were unlike any other known skeletal remains. Scientists named them Neandertals.

A few weeks later, the limestone excavation was finished. Fuhlrott took the bones home to inspect them. He studied the skull. Unlike the skull of a normal human, which has a strong chin and high forehead, this skull had no chin and angled back low over the brain. The face jutted forward beneath the eyes, making the cheekbones angle to the side rather than face forward as ours do. A bulging ridge over the eyes and a bulge at the base completed the strange skull.

The other bones were big and thick and included thigh bones that curved. Fuhlrott knew that whatever this strange creature was, it was no cave bear. Laying the bones out to form a skeleton, Fuhlrott believed that what he was looking at were the remains of an ancient human.

This skull of a Neandertal shows the characteristic ridge over the eyes and the cheekbones angling more to the side than forward.

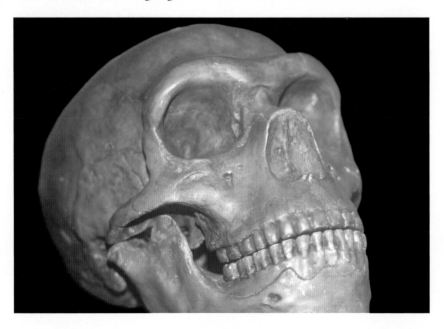

The Name Game

Neandertals have been surrounded by controversy since the first skeleton was hauled out of a cave in the 1850s. People even disagree over the spelling of their name. At the time that Neandertals were named, thal, or valley, was spelled with an h in German. In modern German, it is spelled tal. The h has been dropped. Some scientists prefer the original spelling. This book uses the modern spelling, Neandertal. Both spellings are pronounced the same way, however, as German has no soft th sound. The last syllable is always pronounced tal with a hard t, as in Tom.

He asked some scientists about the bones. One thought that they were just the remains of a hermit or of a feeble-minded person who had wandered off. Another, noting the skeleton's heavy, bowed legs, declared the skeleton's owner to be a Mongolian cavalry soldier who had suffered from rickets.

Others, who were fascinated by a new theory called evolution, declared the skeleton to be the "missing link" between apes and humans. The skeleton eventually went to the laboratory of an expert in anatomy, who recognized it as an ancient human. But, added a fellow anatomist, "were this the skeleton of the oldest man, then the oldest man was a freak."

Soon more skeletons with the same strange features were found in other parts of Europe. They became known as Neandertals after the place that first skeleton was found—the Neander Valley, or Neander *tal* in German.

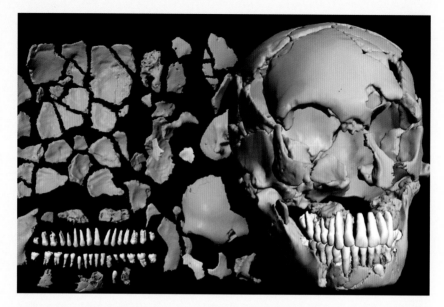

New computer technology allows Neandertal fossils to be scanned and then digitally disassembled so that scientists can study each individual bone.

Thus began the long and strange journey of Neandertal man, the best known, least understood, and most controversial of our predecessors.

NEANDERTAL STUDY

Neandertals are the most studied group of fossil hominids, or members of the human lineage. Their discovery ushered in the modern field of paleoanthropology, the study of human fossils. Since the 1950s, scientists have been sketching the picture of Neandertals and their world. Since the 1980s, new finds, dating techniques, computer technologies, and DNA studies have allowed researchers to fill in the picture.

The Scientists Who Study Neandertals

This book refers, in a very general way, to the "researchers" and "scientists" involved in the study of Neandertals. But many types of scientists have made it their life's work to understand the history of human life on Earth, including Neandertals and other hominids. These scientists are most involved in the study of Neandertals:

An *anthropologist* studies all aspects of human behavior, including culture, language, art, and human biology and evolution. Some anthropologists specialize in certain fields. A *physical anthropologist*, for example, studies human remains to learn about human history and biology. An *evolutionary anthropologist* studies the evolution of hominids. A *paleoanthropologist* studies early humans by excavating skeletal remains and artifacts.

Although their work overlaps, the field of an *archaeologist* is a little narrower than that of an anthropologist. An archaeologist studies material culture—artifacts, buildings, tools, and other objects people have thrown out or left behind—to understand human cultures of the past. An archaeologist is like a detective who uses tools and scientific methods to dig in the ground and recover clues about people of the past.

A *paleontologist* studies fossil remains of plant and animal life on Earth. A paleontologist does not usually deal with human skeletons and artifacts, but paleontologists and archaeologists can work together. For example, a paleontologist might study the animal bones and plant pollen found at a Neandertal site to help archaeologists determine what the people ate.

Paleontologists chip away at a rock face in Madagascar.

Scientists use fossil records to determine what Neandertals looked like, where they lived, and when. Artifacts buried with the skeletons show what tools and other material goods they had, what foods they ate, and some clues to how they lived. Geological records tell about the world in which the Neandertals lived—how cold it was, what the terrain was like, and what plants and animals coexisted with them. DNA studies are beginning to unravel the mystery of whether the Neandertals are related to us in any way.

NEANDERTAL DEBATE

More than 150 years after the first Neandertal skeleton was discovered, researchers are still debating—sometimes bitterly—who these ancient people were, how much like us they were, and what happened to them. Scientists don't even agree on whether Neandertals were a separate species (*Homo neanderthalensis*) or a subspecies (*Homo sapiens neanderthalensis*) of our own species (*Homo sapiens*).

There are two facts that scientists can agree on. One is that Neandertals were short, powerful people who lived in Europe and western Asia for more than two hundred thousand years. The second fact is that they disappeared around twenty-eight thousand years ago, ten thousand years or more after *Homo sapiens* arrived in Europe. That's where the debate begins. What happened to the Neandertals? Maybe Neandertals evolved to look more like early modern humans. Maybe the Neandertals had children with early modern humans, but their genes were "swamped," or overpowered, by the genes of modern humans. Or maybe Neandertals and early modern humans were so different they didn't or couldn't have children together.

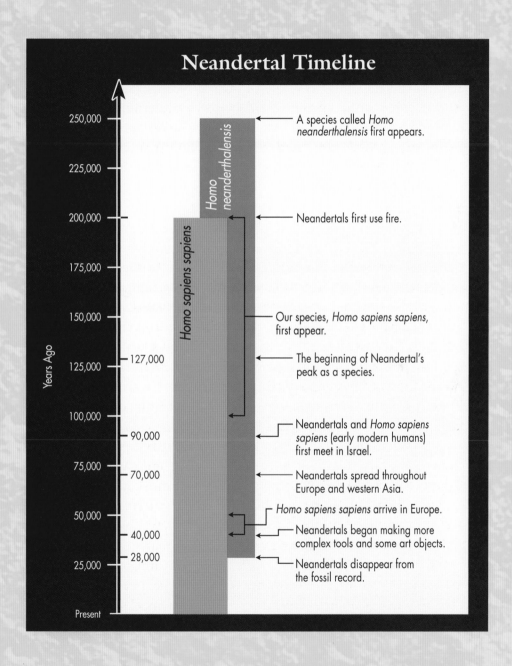

Neandertal Timeline

Years Ago

250,000 — A species called *Homo neanderthalensis* first appears.

225,000

Homo neanderthalensis

200,000 — Neandertals first use fire.

175,000

Homo sapiens sapiens

150,000 — Our species, *Homo sapiens sapiens*, first appear.

127,000 — The beginning of Neandertal's peak as a species.

125,000

100,000

90,000 — Neandertals and *Homo sapiens sapiens* (early modern humans) first meet in Israel.

75,000

70,000 — Neandertals spread throughout Europe and western Asia.

50,000 — *Homo sapiens sapiens* arrive in Europe.

40,000 — Neandertals began making more complex tools and some art objects.

28,000 — Neandertals disappear from the fossil record.

25,000

Present

Maybe early moderns killed the Neandertals instead through violence or by infecting them with disease.

What scientists think occurred when Neandertals met early modern humans depends on what they think Neandertals were like. And how researchers have viewed Neandertals has changed dramatically over the years, from dumb hulking beasts to sensitive family men to . . . well, it depends on whom you ask. Even in the twenty-first century, scientists can't agree on exactly who the Neandertals were—ancestors, brothers and sisters, or distant cousins of modern humans.

It may seem strange that scientists have such a hard time agreeing on Neandertals. Since they're all studying the same skeletons and tools, they should see the same thing, right? It's not as easy as that. Scientists read the bones and artifacts for clues to Neandertal identity and behavior. But depending on how scientists read the bones—what they're looking for, what opinions they've already formed about Neandertals—the bones tell different stories. The debate gets passionate because behind the argument over what happened to the Neandertals lurk questions about ourselves: what does it mean to be human, and why are we the lone surviving human species?

CHAPTER ONE
DISCOVERY

The bones of the original Neandertal skeleton include a skullcap and bones of the leg, hip, and arm.

The Neander Valley skeleton eventually made its way from the hands of the amateur natural historian Johann Fuhlrott to a recognized expert. Hermann Schaafhausen was a German scientist who specialized in human anatomy. He studied the skull with its heavy eyebrows and bulge at the back. He pondered the thick, curved, apelike limbs of the skeleton. Where most other scientists saw a misshapen or diseased freak, Schaafhausen saw the remains of a primitive man. Schaafhausen was perhaps more inclined to

A physician and a professor of anatomy at the University of Bonn in Germany, Hermann Schaafhausen (1816–1893) was the first expert to study the Neander Valley skeleton and determine that the bones were those of an ancient man. This conclusion was not popular with his peers, who didn't support the theory of evolution.

see an ancient human because he, unlike most people of his time, was impressed by the radical new theory of evolution.

EVOLUTION AND NATURAL SELECTION

Just three years after the Neander skeleton was unearthed, Charles Darwin published the revolutionary book *On the Origin of Species*. People recognized at the time that certain traits, such as a straight nose or green eyes, could be inherited, or passed on from generation to generation. But most Europeans believed that the basic human form and mind had been laid down by a divine plan—that is, by God—and didn't change.

In his book, Darwin described how different plants and animals evolved, or developed and changed, over hundreds of thousands of years. Though others had been struggling with the ideas of evolution for years, Darwin laid out the surprisingly simple means by which it happens: natural selection. Darwin noticed that many types of plants and animals were similar but not identical. For example, a bird living on the mainland was slightly different from its counterpart on an island. Or a plant growing on top of a mountain differed from a similar one growing down in a valley. This observation led him to suspect that living things changed over great periods of time as they adapted to their habitats. Natural selection basically means that the individuals of a population that are best able to find food, avoid predators (animals that want to eat them), and reproduce are the ones that survive. Whatever trait or traits those individuals have that allow them to survive get passed down to the next generation. In that way, certain traits are "selected." Individuals with traits that make them less suited for survival die and don't pass on those traits to their offspring. Those traits eventually disappear from the population. Here's an example: Suppose a certain type of lizard lives on the mainland covered with green plants. Most of the lizards of this type are green, which allows them to blend into the background and avoid

The evolutionary theory of British scientist Charles Darwin (right) (1809–1882) as presented in On the Origin of Species *was a major influence on modern scientific thought.*

Evolution: Theory or Fact?

Actually, it's both. Biological evolution is a fact. It is a process that has gone on throughout the history of Earth and one that can be demonstrated. Biologists, however, are less certain of the exact way evolution occurs. They have several theories of the mechanism of evolution. Many people mistakenly believe that a theory is the same thing as a guess. Actually, a theory is a well-supported explanation based on confirmed observations. And facts are not questioned even if scientists debate rival theories to explain them. Darwin accomplished two things: he established the fact of evolution, and he proposed a theory, natural selection, to explain the mechanism that brings it about. Nothing has disproved the Darwinian theory of evolution since it was proposed about 150 years ago. It has withstood the test of time and thousands of scientific experiments, although some people—known as creationists—still dispute the theory.

predators. Occasionally one is born brown. Those lizards are easily spotted and eaten, so very few survive long enough to reproduce and pass on their brown trait. Imagine that a group of these lizards climbs aboard a log that floats across the water to an island. This island is mostly covered in brown rock and has few green plants. As the island population of lizards reproduces, the occasional brown lizard is better suited to avoiding predators. The green lizards, on the other hand, stand out as targets for predators in that environment. Over thousands of generations, the brown lizards survive and reproduce. They pass on the brown trait and perhaps other traits that help them survive in the island habitat. Because green lizards get eaten by predators, the green trait disappears. Eventually, the two populations of lizards—those on the mainland and those on the island—become so different that they are considered different species. Multiplied over millions of generations, this process of natural selection can explain all the different species of living things on Earth.

MISSING LINK

Darwin believed that humans had evolved from earlier forms, just as all plants and animals had. But he was careful not to say so in his book. He was afraid that the idea of human evolution would be so upsetting to his readers that they wouldn't accept the general idea of evolution. But the similarities between humans and apes had long been noted. So other people naturally extended the theory of evolution to include humans. What was needed to prove human evolution was a skeleton that looked like a transition from apes to humans: the "missing link" in the chain of change from ape to human. And the skeleton from the Neander Valley seemed to fill the bill perfectly. Many supporters of the theory of human evolution hailed the Neander man as the missing link.

This illustration shows hypothetical human evolution starting with an African ape (left) *and finally showing a modern human* (right).

Many others, particularly critics of the idea of human evolution, continued to dismiss the Neander skeleton as simply the remains of a diseased man from the Middle Ages (about A.D 500 to about 1500). By denying the evidence of an ancient human, critics hoped to squelch the whole idea of human evolution.

NOT MY ANCESTOR!

Over the years, people found more skeletons with the same strange features in other parts of Europe, including Belgium and France. And earlier finds of a child's skull in 1829 and a female skull in 1848 were then identified as Neandertal. Some of these skeletons were obviously ancient because they were buried with stone tools and the bones of mammals that had become extinct, or died out, thousands of years before. Then, at the beginning of the twentieth century, the bones of as many as eighty Neandertals were discovered in a cave in Croatia in eastern Europe. With all this evidence, it was clear that Neandertals were not diseased hermits but were humanlike creatures that had lived thousands of years ago. Scientists determined that their skulls would have held brains of our size and that they were more like humans than apes. They may have even evolved into one of the modern human races. Many scientists accepted Neandertals as a type of *Homo sapiens.*

Though they could accept Neandertals as an ancient human race, there were those who just could not accept the idea of Neandertals as direct ancestors of modern Europeans. Neandertals were just too primitive looking, with those menacing browridges and thick, curved limbs. They might be somebody's ancestor, many Europeans thought, but not theirs. They could imagine Neandertals having evolved into what they considered to be a more "primitive people," such as the Aborigines of Australia. But to go from this simple cave dweller to the educated and enlightened European of the late nineteenth century? That would mean that relatively little separated the cave dweller from the modern European. Unthinkable!

A few Europeans, however, could think of Neandertal man as one of them. An illustration in the popular magazine *Harper's Weekly* in 1873 showed a Neandertal man standing upright with an intelligent look on his face. He wore primitive clothes and had a dog by his side. He warmed himself with a cozy fire and possessed fine tools.

If this image of Neandertal man had caught on, "Neanderthal!" would never have become an insult to yell at the bully on the playground. But in 1908, the French paleontologist Marcellin Boule got hold of a Neandertal skeleton. From his studies, a very different picture emerged. It was just the beginning of the hundred-year battle to determine where to draw the line between modern humans and our prehuman ancestors—a battle that continues in the twenty-first century.

The 1873 illustration of a Neandertal man from Harper's Weekly

CHAPTER TWO
THE FEARSOME CREATURE

In 1908 three Catholic priests discovered a Neandertal skeleton in a cave near a church at La Chapelle-aux-Saints in southern France. It was the most complete Neandertal skeleton yet discovered and included most of the backbone.

By that time, the debate on human evolution had intensified. Some people accepted the biblical story of God creating Adam and Eve as the first humans and therefore did not believe in evolution at all. Some, including the priests who found the skeleton, sought a compromise between science and religion. They accepted the theory of evolution but not the idea that a creature as primitive as a Neandertal could have evolved into modern Europeans. Others, known as combat anthropologists, openly struggled against church teachings. They believed in a straight line of evolution, or linear evolution, from apes to ancient humans like Neandertals to modern humans.

Had the La Chapelle skeleton ended up in the hands of one of the combat anthropologists for study, the story of Neandertals would have been very different. But the priests wanted the skeleton to go to a more conservative scientist with ties to the Roman Catholic Church. They chose Marcellin Boule, the leading paleontologist in France.

This skeleton, discovered in 1908 in the village of La Chapelle-aux-Saints in southern France, wound up in the hands of French paleontologist Marcellin Boule—much to the detriment of the species' reputation. Boule portrayed Neandertals as shuffling, hairy creatures of low intellect, a description that lived long after it was disproved.

(23)

BOULE AND THE OLD MAN OF LA CHAPELLE

Boule believed in evolution, but he did not believe there was a linear descent from apes to us. Instead, he believed that evolution was more like a tree, with lots of branches that led to dead ends. He believed that Neandertal man was one of those side branches that led nowhere. And even if it were to lead somewhere, it would certainly not be to modern Europeans.

To support his treelike version of evolution, he had to characterize the skeleton as something very different from a modern human. He had to paint a picture of Neandertal man that was so different that it had gone extinct, probably at the hands of our true ancestor.

With this goal in mind, Boule read the bones of the Old Man of La Chapelle, as the skeleton had been nicknamed, and saw something even more primitive than earlier scientists had. After studying the skull, he acknowledged that the Old Man's brain was as big as the average Frenchman's, but he said it lacked volume in exactly the areas needed for higher intelligence. Neandertals, he concluded, would have been smart enough only to make very simple, crude tools.

He studied the backbone and determined that the Old Man could barely stand upright. Instead, he walked stooped over, knees bent, knuckles grazing the ground. Boule described the Old Man's head as slung forward on a short, thick neck. He even concluded that the Neandertal couldn't smile because his face muscles were too tight.

The main point of Boule's description was to firmly boot Neandertals out of our family tree and establish them as a separate species—*Homo neanderthalensis*.

In 1909 an illustration of the Old Man of La Chapelle based on Boule's findings was published in a French newspaper.

Marcellin Boule

Marcellin Boule was born January 1, 1861, in France. He was a geologist, paleontologist, and physical anthropologist who studied human fossils from all over the world. He became the director of the Laboratory of Paleontology and the important Natural History Museum in Paris. His reconstruction of the skeleton from La Chapelle-aux-Saints in 1908 was the first of its kind for Neandertals. And his report on the Old Man of La Chapelle was the most complete report on Neandertals since the first skeleton was discovered in 1856. In later years, he made a name for himself for his work on the Piltdown man, described in the next chapter. Boule died on July 4, 1942.

Marcellin Boule was the first to reconstruct a Neandertal skeleton.

Based on the work of Marcellin Boule, this illustration of the Old Man of La Chapelle was published in the French newspaper L'Illustration *in 1909 and in the* Illustrated London News *about a week later.*

The picture in *L'Illustration* is a striking contrast to the one shown on page 21, published in *Harper's Weekly* about thirty-six years earlier. Gone are the cozy fire, human-made tools and clothes, companion dog, and thoughtful man. In this illustration, a stooped, hairy creature clutches a crude club in one hand and a rock in the other. The only thing he looks capable of is bashing in the heads of animals. The bones of his prey litter the floor at his feet. People reading this newspaper would clearly have had a difficult time imagining this brute as their ancestor.

SCOWLING BEAST OR SENSITIVE ANCESTOR?

Not all newspapers, however, accepted Boule's characterization of Neandertals. Newspapers that supported linear evolution continued to show a more human Neandertal man as the missing link. In 1911 the *Illustrated London News* published another very different image of the Old Man of La Chapelle. This illustration was

This illustration of the Old Man of La Chapelle was published in the Illustrated London News *in 1911.*

A protégé of Charles Darwin, Scottish anatomist and physical anthropologist Sir Arthur Keith (1866–1955) specialized in the study of the fossils of early humans.

also based on an expert's description. This time the expert was Arthur Keith, a Scottish anthropologist who disagreed with Boule. This illustration once again shows a human-looking Neandertal, deep in thought, as he sits by a fire skillfully making a tool. The man wears a fur skirt and necklace, his spear propped nearby.

Both illustrations were approved by respected scientists and supposedly represented unbiased scientific fact. But in reality, much of the research regarding Neandertals at the time was less about Neandertals and more about defending existing positions on evolution. Scientists used public newspapers to air their prejudices. The public's view of Neandertals depended on whether people read a conservative, antievolution paper or a more progressive one. According to newspaper accounts, either Neandertals were intelligent ancient humans just a step away from modern Europeans or a vastly inferior evolutionary side branch that was too brutish to do anything but go extinct. Those were the two choices presented to the public.

SCOWLING BEAST WINS

Eventually it was Boule's scowling beast that triumphed. Though many Europeans at the time could accept the idea of human evolution in theory, it was harder to be faced with an actual primitive ancestor. It was more comforting to believe that an ancient ancestor was out there, but this beetle-browed man wasn't it. It also didn't help the Neandertals' case that Arthur Keith later changed his mind and supported Boule's position.

Another blow knocking Neandertals out of our family tree was the discovery around 1912 of the skull of another ancient man in Sussex County, England. Piltdown man, as he was called, was found with some mastodon teeth as well as bones of other extinct animals, so it was clearly ancient. The skull had an

This is a reconstruction of the skull of Piltdown man, found around 1912 in Great Britain.

apelike jaw, but the rest was more human looking. It didn't have the low, sloping forehead and heavy brows that made the Neandertals look so primitive. Here was an ancient man older than Neandertals yet with a more modern look. It was a much more acceptable ancestor. Some U.S. scientists questioned the authenticity of the skull. They thought the jaw and skullcap seemed too different to belong to the same individual. When a second Piltdown man was found in 1915, many scientists, including Boule at first, declared it our earliest ancestor.

This is a bust of what Piltdown man would have looked like, based on the skull that was found in 1912.

Neandertal man's brutish reputation was by then cemented in the public's imagination. Here's how British writer H. G. Wells described Neandertals in 1921: "Hairy or grisly, with a big face like a mask, great browridges and no forehead, clutching an enormous flint, and running like a baboon with his head forward and not, like a man, with his head up, he must have been a fearsome creature for our forefathers to come upon."

In modern times, when we think of Neandertals, most of us still picture the stooped beast described by Boule. Cartoons, movies, and even some museums have portrayed Neandertal man as a hairy creature hulking over a tiny fire or clubbing his mate over the head and dragging her back to his cave.

So scientists continued looking for more suitable ancestors, and Neandertals were forgotten for the next fifty years.

In the mid-twentieth century, several new finds revived interest in the long-forgotten and much misunderstood Neandertals. In 1939 construction workers outside Rome, Italy, broke into a cave that had been sealed for fifty thousand years. Inside was a single skull of a Neandertal, circled by carefully placed rocks. This was evidence of a ritual burial. It suggested that Neandertals believed in an afterlife. A few researchers were interested in this discovery.

Then, in 1953, Piltdown man, the seemingly perfect missing link, was recognized by the scientific community as a fake. It was actually the work of Marcellin Boule that helped expose that someone had cleverly buried the lower jawbone of an ape with the skull of a modern man and some animal bones to make the remains look ancient. Whoever played this archaeological joke fooled a lot of experts for almost forty years. The hunt for the missing link was back on.

For modern scientists, one measure of the "humanness" of ancient people was their ability—and interest— in creating art. For a long time, no jewelry, carvings, or other pieces of art from Neandertal culture were found. Scientists didn't think Neandertals had the intelligence or creativity to make items that were purely

Charles Dawson (left) and Sir Arthur Smith-Woodward (right) dig at Piltdown in 1910. The skeleton of Piltdown man that the men found in 1912 was proven to be a fake in 1953, thus reawakening interest in Neandertal research.

for pleasure. But in 1958, researchers in Hungary found a carved and polished ivory tooth from a baby mammoth. The tooth, which was between eighty thousand and one hundred thousand years old, didn't appear to have any practical use. Yet someone had worked hard to make it smooth and shiny. Because modern humans had not arrived in Europe yet, researchers know that that someone had to have been a Neandertal.

PREHISTORIC FLOWER PEOPLE

In the late 1950s, scientists excavated a large cave called Shanidar in Iraq. Inside they found the skeletons of nine Neandertals buried about sixty thousand years ago. In one grave, a man, two women, and an infant were buried together. The excavators also found the fossilized pollen of early spring wildflowers in the soil around some of the skeletons.

Below is a skull from one of the nine Neandertal skeletons found in Shanidar Cave in Iraq in the 1950s.

Luckily for the Neandertals, the 1950s and 1960s were a good time for scientists to rethink their views on these ancient people. Early researchers had focused on how Neandertals looked. They decided from that evidence alone that Neandertals must have been dumb savages. In the era of civil rights beginning in the United States in the 1950s, people no longer felt it was right to judge a group's capabilities simply on their physical features. Scientists began to focus less on Neandertal anatomy and began to look for clues to their behavior. They started with the Shanidar skeletons.

The first of the nine skeletons unearthed was formally called Shanidar 1 but nicknamed Nandy. Nandy was injured from head to toe. During his life, he had been smashed over the head. The blow left him with a crushed cheek and blind in one eye.

This illustration, done for National Geographic magazine in 1996, based on the first Shanidar skeleton, nicknamed Nandy, shows the injured Neandertal being helped by a young Neandertal boy.

A Dangerous Life

By looking at their bones, scientists can tell that Neandertals led very hard and very dangerous lives. Most skeletons of adult Neandertals show evidence of at least one broken bone or other injury. Many have several severe injuries, such as broken ribs, legs, and spines, head injuries, and stab wounds. Often these injuries resulted in death. Researchers compared the number and extent of Neandertal injuries with those of modern people. Only one group came close to matching the tough life of Neandertals: rodeo riders. Most of Neandertals' severe injuries were due to the way they hunted. They surrounded large animals, such as aurochs, an extinct species of giant cattle, and thrust spears into them. They may have even leaped onto their prey to stab them or wrestle them to the ground. This behavior put them right in harm's way.

Most Neandertals who lived to be close to forty also suffered from arthritis in their ankles, spines, hips, knees, fingers, or toes. Arthritis is an inflammation of the joints that is most commonly caused by wear and tear. The Neandertal lifestyle resulted in plenty of wear and tear. They walked long distances in search of food and toolmaking materials, which was hard on their backs, hips, knees, and feet. Repetitive motions from toolmaking, scraping hides, and other activities was hard on their fingers.

Arthritis is still common. Virtually all of us, if we live long enough, will develop it in one or more of our joints.

He had broken his arm in two places above the elbow. The fractures hadn't healed correctly, and eventually his arm had withered away. Nandy limped painfully on his right foot, which had a healed fracture on the outside as well as severe arthritis in the ankle and big toe. Despite these injuries, Nandy lived to the ripe old age of about forty at a time when Neandertals seldom lived past thirty. With all those injuries,

Nandy would not have been able to hunt and find food for himself. Obviously, the members of his group had tended to his wounds, perhaps using plants and herbs with healing properties. They also fed and protected him and helped him move about.

Nandy wasn't the only Neandertal to receive care and attention from his group. Shanidar 3, who also died when he was around forty, lived for several weeks after surviving a chest wound so deep that it marked one of his rib bones. He also had arthritis in his foot severe enough to cause him to limp painfully. Although he may have eventually died as a result of the chest wound, that he survived for several weeks indicates that, like Nandy, he was taken care of by someone.

Excavators found pollen grains under the skeleton of Shanidar 4. The grains appeared to be in a pattern, as if wildflowers had been carefully arranged under the body during burial. Scientists found it interesting too that most of the flowers,

Some scientists see evidence that Neandertals intentionally buried their dead, very likely with some ritual as shown in the illustration.

such as yarrow and hollyhock, have been used in the past as medicine.

The scientist in charge of the excavation, Ralph S. Solecki, published a book about the Shanidar Neandertals in 1971. It was called *Shanidar: The First Flower People.* Suddenly Neandertals went from being viewed as fearsome creatures to sensitive flower lovers.

BONES TELL A NEW STORY

In 1957, with their eyes and minds open, scientists returned to some of the first Neandertal skeletons and found that the skeletons had a very different story to tell. It turns out that the Old Man of La Chapelle, whom Marcellin Boule had dismissed as a stooping beast, was an old man (by Neandertal standards) who had suffered from severe arthritis in his hip and spine. That was why his thigh bones and backbone were curved, causing him to stoop. He had lost most of his teeth to gum disease. He would not have been able to hunt. In fact, he would have had trouble simply walking and chewing his food. Yet he lived to be around forty, so someone must have helped him. There's evidence that Boule knew that the Old Man's curved posture was due to arthritis but ignored this because it didn't support the story he wanted to tell about Neandertals.

Even the famous Neander Valley Neandertal man overcame numerous injuries. He would not have been able to use his left arm properly after a bad break and probably had to do everything with his right arm. And he, too, suffered from arthritis.

From these new studies, a new picture of Neandertals began to emerge. Perhaps they weren't dumb, insensitive brutes after all. They were people who lived in groups, probably extended

Double Wise Man

People are classified as *Homo sapiens sapiens*. This means we are the subspecies *sapiens* of the species *Homo sapiens*. The first *Homo sapiens* evolved about 500,000 years ago. *Homo sapiens sapiens*, or modern humans, began to appear between 100,000 and 200,000 years ago. They used tools similar to those of the early Neandertals. Modern humans generally have more delicate skeletons than earlier *Homo sapiens*. Our skulls are more rounded and our browridges less prominent.

We are the only remaining subspecies of *Homo sapiens*, which means "wise man." Perhaps that's why we've dubbed ourselves "wise wise man." Scientists who classify Neandertals as *Homo sapiens neanderthalensis* believe that Neandertals are a subspecies of *Homo sapiens*. But most modern scientists classify Neandertals as *Homo neanderthalensis*, which means they believe that Neandertals are a separate species.

families. They cared for one another while they were living and after they had died. By the end of the 1970s, Neandertals were recast as people only slightly different from us and heartily welcomed back into our family tree. Neandertals and modern humans were considered so similar that in 1964 scientists proposed classifying them as two forms of the same species—*Homo sapiens neanderthalensis and Homo sapiens sapiens*. This classification was generally accepted into the 1980s.

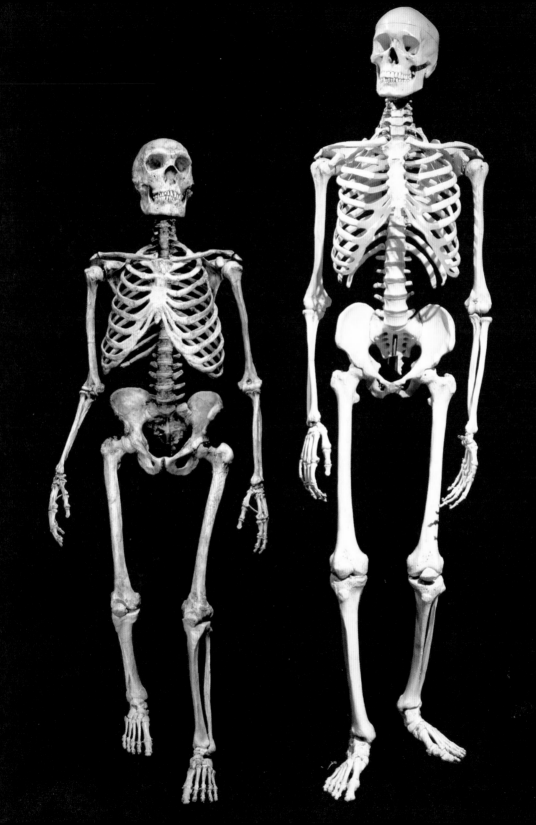

CHAPTER FOUR
OUT OF AFRICA ... AND THE FAMILY TREE: THE 1980S

From the beginning of Neandertal study, experts debated whether Neandertals belonged in our family tree or not. Did Neandertals evolve into modern humans? The idea of a world where two or more human species coexisted seems more like science fiction than reality, but is it possible that Neandertals were a separate species that died off when early modern humans arrived?

By the end of the 1970s, Neandertals were tentatively perched in our family tree. At the time, the linear model of human evolution seemed to make the most sense: One ancient hominid species evolved into the next slightly more human species and so on down the line, until Neandertals evolved into modern humans. All hominids that lived before modern humans evolved are called archaic humans, meaning they come from an earlier or more primitive time.

NEANDERTAL, MODERN HUMAN, OR BOTH?

The fossil record in some places, such as eastern Europe, seemed to support a gradual change from the short, robust skeletons of Neandertals to the slender, long-limbed moderns.

The Neandertal skeleton (at far left) was made by piecing together different parts of many different Neandertal skeletons. In comparison to the modern human skeleton (right), note the Neandertal's larger bell-shaped chest cavity and wider pelvis.

The Fossil Record

The fossil record consists of all remnants or traces of organisms that were once alive that are known to scientists. Unfortunately, the fossil record is far from complete, considering how many organisms have lived throughout the history of Earth. The record is incomplete because the chances of an organism becoming fossilized are rare; most fossils are destroyed by environmental conditions, natural processes, and human activities; and only a fraction of surviving fossils will ever be found. For example, some environments, such as tropical rain forests, are particularly bad for fossil formation. In such wet places, dead creatures decay before they get a chance to fossilize. Also, large bones tend to preserve easier. That means that we have more information about large animals in the fossil record than small ones. Of the creatures that do manage to fossilize, only a fraction will ever be found. Fossils are destroyed by natural processes such as rock slides or by building projects. Some fossils may be in outcrops of rocks that are impossible to reach. And some may be in countries where international researchers are not welcome. According to some studies, scientists have discovered less than 10 percent of the existing fossils of primates, which includes humans and their ancestors as well as apes, monkeys, and lemurs.

Scientists found skeletons that appeared to have both Neandertal and modern physical traits.

Then, in the 1980s, archaeologists unearthed a group of skeletons on Mount Carmel in northern Israel. The skeletons were confusing because some appeared to be archaic human skeletons and some appeared to be modern human skeletons. Scientists dated the bones of the different skeletons and determined that they had lived during the same time period. But some were stocky like Neandertals and some slender like mod-

The Neandertals excavated from Mount Carmel in Israel in the 1980s (left) *were found amongst Homo sapien skeletons, making the linear theory of evolution suspect.*

ern humans. If they were living in the same place at the same time, some scientists said, then they must have been the same people. The only difference was their physical build. Just as some modern people are tall and slender and others short and stocky, some *Homo sapiens* were tall and some short.

No, said other scientists, this was evidence that modern humans and Neandertals were two separate species of humans that lived at the same time. And if there were modern humans living at the same time as Neandertals, then Neandertals could not have evolved into modern humans. New finds and dating techniques were also turning up modern human skeletons that were older than some Neandertal skeletons.

Some scientists began to question how researchers in the earlier decades had interpreted Neandertal burial sites. They argued that the skull and rocks at the burial site found in Italy in 1939 had not been carefully arranged but washed into a random pattern by water. And the flower pollen around the skeleton of Shanidar 4 could have just blown in or been brought in by bees that lived in caves around the area. These scientists saw no evidence of the modern human tradition of ritual burials

An artist's rendition of what life might have been like with Neandertals and Homo sapiens living at the same time.

among Neandertals. They began to question whether Neandertals could organize a hunt, build a decent fire, talk, or feel much emotion. All this controversy served to once again nudge Neandertals out of our family tree.

THE MOTHER OF THE HUMAN RACE

Then came Eve.

In 1987 scientists published the results of a study comparing a particular kind of DNA found in cell parts called mitochondria. Mitochondrial DNA is inherited only from mothers and is passed on from generation to generation. It plays no role in determining what we look like, but it does contain a record of our ancestry. The scientists looked at groups of people from all over the world and found that everybody's mitochondrial DNA is very similar. According to the scientists, this means that all Earth's current inhabitants descended from just one ancient hominid, whom they nicknamed Eve, after the biblical first female. We all have similar mitochondrial DNA because Eve is the mother of the whole human race. Furthermore, the scientists concluded that Eve came from Africa because Africans are more genetically diverse than people from other parts of the world. This diversity suggests that Africans have been around longer and thus have had longer for their genes to change from generation to generation.

OUT-OF-AFRICA THEORY

From this one study, most scientists came to accept a new theory of human evolution: Our line of ancestors split off from apes about seven million years ago in Africa. Our ancestors lived in Africa for around five million years and evolved into *Homo erectus.*

Mitochondrial DNA

When the subject of human DNA comes up, most people think of the forty-six chromosomes in the nucleus of almost every cell in our bodies. These chromosomes hold most of the genetic information inherited from parents that determine a lot about us, such as hair color and height. But we all have a small amount of DNA in structures called mitochondria that lie outside the nucleus but still within the cell. Mitochondrial DNA, or mtDNA for short, can't tell us anything about a person's phys-

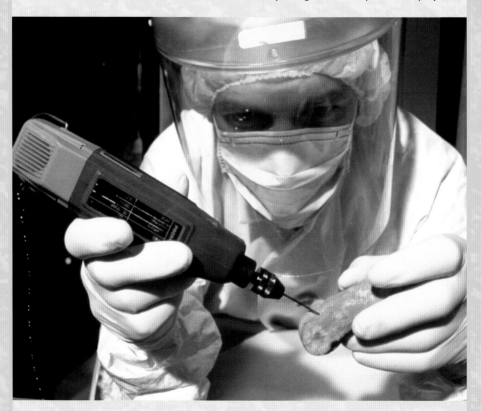

A technician prepares a sample of bone from a Neandertal fossil. A DNA sample will be taken from the bone and analyzed.

ical traits, but scientists can use it to trace the evolution of human species. Mitochondrial DNA is useful to scientists in tracing ancestors for two reasons.

First, mtDNA allows scientists to track ancestors directly because it is only passed on from mothers. When an egg is fertilized, it receives nuclear DNA from both the mother and the father and an exact copy of the mother's mtDNA, but none of the father's mtDNA. This means that all the mtDNA in a person is an exact copy of his or her mother's mtDNA, which is an exact copy of her mother's mtDNA, and so on back through a chain of only mothers. Nuclear DNA, on the other hand, is a muddle of chromosomes inherited from two parents, who in turn inherited it from four grandparents, eight great-grandparents, and so on.

That doesn't mean, however, that your mtDNA is exactly like your direct ancestor's who lived one hundred years ago. Along the way, the mtDNA has been mutating, or changing. The second reason that mtDNA is so useful to evolutionary scientists is that these changes happen at a steady rate. A scientist can compare the mtDNA of living people with the mtDNA of a hominid of long ago to determine when they shared a common ancestor. Say, for example, that the two mtDNAs differed by ten mutations and that the scientist knew the mutation rate to be one in every one thousand years. That would mean that the common ancestor lived ten thousand years ago.

Researchers have compared mtDNA from Neandertal bones with mtDNA from living people around the world and determined that the most recent common ancestor of Neandertals and *Homo sapiens* lived five hundred thousand years ago. That's long before the most recent common ancestor of all living people, Eve, who scientists estimate lived two hundred thousand years ago. This suggests that Neandertals died out without contributing their mtDNA to modern humans, but mtDNA studies are not foolproof, and scientists debate their value.

Modern Humans

Two or three million years ago, one group of hominids in Africa discovered how to make stone tools. They used these tools to cut meat and scrape skins from the animals they killed. As they produced and used more tools, their brains grew. Scientists group these larger-brained hominids into the genus *Homo*. There were many hominids in the *Homo* line, such as *Homo habilis, Homo erectus, Homo sapiens*, and possibly other archaic hominids that we may not have discovered yet.

We belong to the species *Homo sapiens sapiens*. *Homo sapiens sapiens* came on the scene between one hundred thousand and two hundred thousand years ago. Scientists place fossil skeletons in this category based not on smarts but on anatomy, or physical traits. The first anatomically modern skeleton was found in a little rock shelter in France called Cro-Magnon, so *Homo sapiens* are sometimes referred to as Cro-Magnons. But Cro-Magnons are just one example of anatomically modern humans. A better term is modern human.

The latest fossil finds in Ethiopia in Africa are evidence that humans who look like us had evolved by 195,000 years ago. But most scientists agree that *Homo sapiens* that acted like us, called behaviorally modern humans, didn't appear for another 150,000 years. Around 40,000 years ago, about the time that they were moving into Europe, early modern humans began making sophisticated tools, creating art, and engaging in rituals on a much larger scale than ever before in human history.

The illustration below compares the skulls of (left to right) *Neandertals*, Homo Erectus, *and* Homo sapiens.

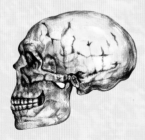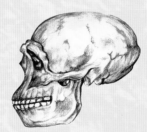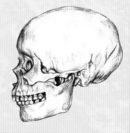

Then, about two million years ago, some populations of *Homo erectus* left Africa and began spreading throughout Europe and Asia. As they adapted to very different environments, they developed different ways of doing things. They even changed physically. The populations eventually changed so much that they became different species. Those in Asia remained *Homo erectus*. Those in Europe evolved into Neandertals between five hundred thousand and three hundred thousand years ago. And those in Africa became *Homo sapiens*, our own species. Then, according to the Out-of-Africa theory, also known as the Replacement Hypothesis, between one hundred thousand and fifty thousand years ago, *Homo sapiens* that were descended from Eve in Africa began spreading throughout Asia and Europe, just as *Homo erectus* had done earlier. This time they encountered other people, including Neandertals. If it is true that all modern people are descended from Eve, then *Homo sapiens* must have somehow replaced all other non-Eve populations, including Neandertals, without interbreeding. The mitochondrial DNA of Neandertals does not resemble DNA from any known modern humans, which is why many scientists believe that the two groups of people did not interbreed.

Replacement theorists find evidence not only in genetic studies of DNA but also in fossils and artifacts. They say that Neandertals looked and behaved so differently from modern humans that they must have been a separate species.

But another camp of scientists maintains that *Homo sapiens* absorbed rather than replaced other archaic humans. According to this model of human evolution, when modern-looking humans from Africa encountered Neandertals, they did not look or act that differently from each other, and the populations interbred.

Our Family Tree

When we first appeared as a species, we shared the planet with lots of other hominids, such as Neandertals, *Homo erectus*, and *Homo habilis*. For more than 150 years, scientists have been collecting bones from all these ancient groups of people and trying to make sense of them. Over the years, scientists have compiled information on a long list of physical traits. These traits include whether the individual walked upright, general body shape and size, the size and shape of the skull and face, brain size, the size and shape of the teeth and jaw, and opposable thumbs. By dating the bones, researchers keep track of when various features appeared and disappeared in groups of people. From this information, they have constructed a many-branched tree that attempts to show how we are related to the different hominids. When a skeleton is found, scientists compare it to the data they have compiled to see to which group it belongs. Occasionally, a skeleton is found that is so unlike any others that it deserves a new classification.

A linear evolution chart, such as the one at left, shows one species directly evolving from another. The family tree is more complicated, showing species evolving independently of one another.

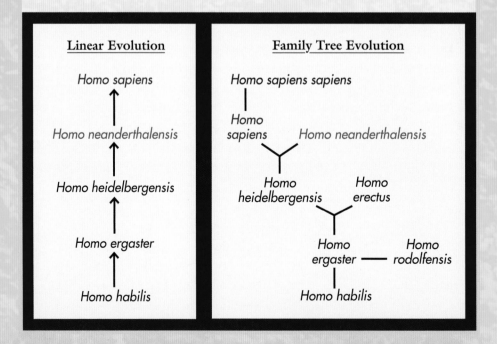

The modern humans had some evolutionary advantage that increased their population, and their genes eventually "swamped" the Neandertal genes. According to this theory, then, Europeans today have a tiny bit of Neandertal lurking in them.

Just as the replacement theorists look to the fossil record for proof, so does the other camp of scientists. There they find evidence that Neandertals were more similar to than different from modern humans.

In the years since the Eve hypothesis was launched, much research has focused on Neandertals. Because Neandertals are the most studied ancient human group, scientists try out the latest technologies in dating and DNA testing on Neandertals as they continue to struggle with the three big questions: Who were the Neandertals? How did they live? What happened to them? Just as in past years, the answers the scientists find often seem to depend on what camp they are in.

CHAPTER FIVE
WHO WERE THEY?
NEANDERTALS AND THEIR WORLD

What makes Neandertals Neandertals is not where and when they lived, how they lived, or even how smart they were. Neandertals are defined by physical characteristics that distinguish them from other human groups. Those physical traits began to appear in the fossil record about 250,000 years ago. There are few fossil remains of these early Neandertals and their artifacts, and almost no record of them after about 180,000 years ago, when glaciers covered Europe. But some hardy Neandertals must have struggled through the bitter cold. By 127,000 years ago, when warmth returned to Europe and the fossil record picks up, Neandertals had developed the classic Neandertal look: short, stocky body with a barrel chest; thick limbs; a skull with a ridge above the eyes; a large nose; and a bulge at the base of the skull called an occipital bun. They also left more tools and artifacts than the earlier Neandertals. These tools showed them to be skilled hunters. This was the beginning of the Neandertal heyday. They ruled ice-age Europe for 200,000 years, or more than ten thousand generations.

Neandertals evolved in western Europe, and by seventy thousand years ago, they had spread throughout Europe and western Asia. Their fossils have been found in almost every country in Europe, from as far north as Great Britain to as far south as Spain, as well as in central Asia and the Middle East. Paleoanthropologists have no idea

A model of a Neandertal man created between 1929 and 1933 at the Field Museum in Chicago, Illinois, shows the classic Neandertal look as determined by early twentieth-century research.

how many Neandertals there were, but there were probably no more than tens of thousands at any one time.

Glaciers repeatedly pushed into and retreated from Europe during their lives. When the glaciers crept in and edible plants became scarce, Neandertals relied less on gathering plants and more on hunting reindeer and wild horses. Neandertals moved as far south as Israel, where it was warmer. In the period between glaciers, Neandertals pushed farther north as the ice sheets shrank. They were probably the first humans to live regularly in bitter cold climates. To do so, they developed tools, clothes, shelter, and fire.

The Last Ice Age

There have been several ice ages in the history of Earth. What is commonly called the Ice Age is actually the most recent one, which began about two million years ago. Sea levels were lower than they are currently because much of the water on Earth was frozen into ice. Snow covered much of the land, and ice sheets extended over large areas. But it wasn't just one long cold snap. Scientists think that there were twenty-one ice ages, or glaciations. In between the glaciations, Earth warmed up. At times thick sheets of ice covered much of present-day Great Britain. At other times, it was warm enough for elephants and hippopotamuses to live in Great Britain.

Many large mammals prowled the land, including saber-toothed cats, giant ground sloths, mastodons, and mammoths. These animals became extinct long ago and are known to us through fossils and ancient cave paintings.

During the last ice age, much of human evolution took place. The Neandertals evolved, flourished, and disappeared. *Homo sapiens* arose, spread from Africa into Europe, developed modern behavior, and became the sole remaining human species.

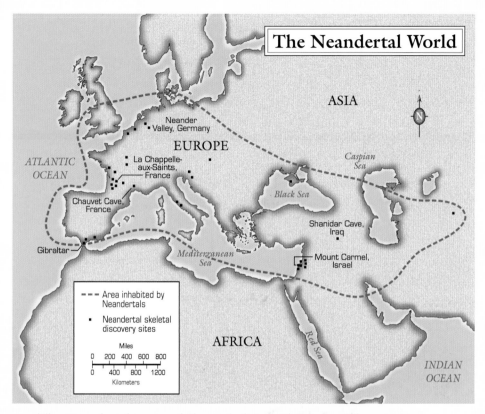

The Neandertals roamed through Asia and Europe. There is no evidence that they ever crossed onto the African continent.

CLASSIC NEANDERTAL LOOK

Not all Neandertals looked exactly alike. Since they lived over a long period of time, throughout a vast region, and during warm and cold times, their appearance varied a great deal. The Neandertals who lived in western Europe seventy thousand years ago until their disappearance around twenty-eight thousand years ago have what's become identified as the classic Neandertal look—the look that defines Neandertals.

In addition to the typical Neandertal's weak chin, sloping forehead, and heavy browridges, the places on the outside of the jaw where chewing muscles were attached are very big, suggesting that Neandertals had a powerful bite. The front teeth of adult Neandertals were worn down, almost to stubs. Apparently, Neandertals used their teeth for more than chewing. They used their front ones like a third hand, to hold objects they were working on. On average, their brains were larger than ours. But having larger brains doesn't necessarily mean people are smarter. In proportion to our lighter bodies, our brains are relatively larger. Neandertals probably needed bigger brains to coordinate their big, heavily muscled bodies. Researchers have tried to tell if Neandertal brains were shaped differently from ours based on

Comparison of early modern human skull (left) *to a Neandertal skull* (right)

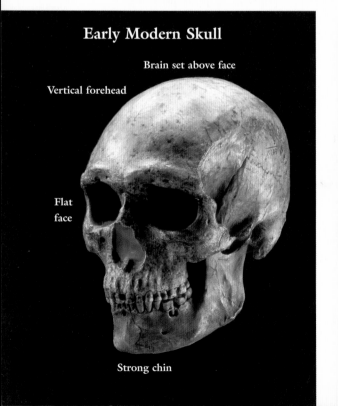

Early Modern Skull

Brain set above face

Vertical forehead

Flat face

Strong chin

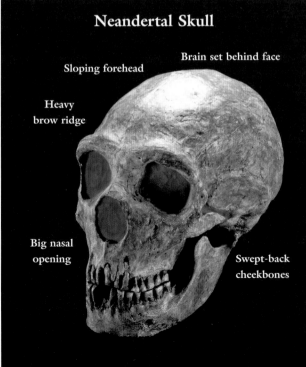

Neandertal Skull

Sloping forehead

Brain set behind face

Heavy brow ridge

Big nasal opening

Swept-back cheekbones

the shape of the inside of their skulls. So far it appears that Neandertal and modern human brains were basically the same shape.

Neandertals were stocky people compared to modern humans. They had long trunks, powerful shoulders, and short, thick limbs. Considering the size of their arms and legs and the marks left on their fossilized bones by muscles, Neandertals must have been incredibly strong. An adult Neandertal man would probably have weighed around 200 pounds (90 kilograms). But their big, bulky bodies did not make them clumsy, as was previously thought. In 2003 researchers proved that Neandertal hands were just like ours. Neandertals could touch index finger to thumb, which would have given them great dexterity.

Neandertal bodies are often compared to the Inuit, indigenous people who have adapted to the cold of the far north. Most researchers agree that classic Neandertal features developed as an adaptation to extremely cold weather. For example, short bodies and limbs conserve heat because there is less surface area from which to lose it. Until recently researchers believed that their big, broad noses also were an adaptation to the cold. A big nose might warm cold, dry air and give it some moisture before it reached the lungs. But studies from 2005 challenge this idea. Researchers found that Neandertals had big noses no matter where they lived—in cold, dry northern Europe or the warm, humid Middle East. Some scientists argue that their big noses were a result of their large upper jaws.

BROTHER OR COUSIN?

All our information about Neandertal anatomy is based on several hundred fossils of Neandertals or their direct ancestors and several nearly complete skeletons. Since there is no complete single skeleton, Neandertal appearance has been open to a certain amount of interpretation. In the past, some scientists argued that you could dress a Neandertal man in modern clothes and put him on a busy New York subway and no one would notice him. Other scientists disagreed.

In 2002 scientists put together the first complete Neandertal skeleton using parts of skeletons found in France, Germany, and Israel. The resulting individual looked very different from a modern human. The skeleton stood just 5 foot 4 inches (163 centimeters) tall, thought to be the typical height of a Neandertal man. Its shoulders and pelvis were extremely wide, its rib cage large and shaped like a bell, and its shins and forearms surprisingly short. Some scientists argue that it's clear from this reconstruction that Neandertals and modern humans had such pronounced physical differences that they must be separate species.

Then, just two years later, a study of Neandertal tooth growth concluded that Neandertals reached adulthood by the age of fifteen, about three years earlier than modern humans normally do. The time it takes for a tooth to grow can be measured by counting visible lines that form on the enamel about every nine days, similar to counting rings on a tree. The finding that Neandertals and modern humans developed at different rates was seen by many as further proof that the two belonged to separate species.

A year later, however, another tooth study found no proof that the two were separate species. The scientists behind the new study said that Neandertals' front teeth grew faster than the teeth of some populations of humans living today but slower than those of others. They concluded that Neandertals' teeth grew at a rate comparable to modern humans. So Neandertals would have enjoyed a long childhood just like early

Homo heidelbergensis: Grandparents of Neandertals

Since the 1980s, archaeologists have unearthed the remains of more than thirty-two individuals from the muddy floors of limestone caves in northern Spain. This place is like a gold mine for archaeologists. The bones date to around three hundred thousand years ago. For many years, scientists lumped the confusing array of human skeletons that didn't look quite modern all together and called them archaic *Homo sapiens* because they did not know what else to call them. Recently, scientists have begun to call this wide range of skeletons, which lived from about eight hundred thousand years ago to the appearance of anatomically modern humans, *Homo heidelbergensis*. *Homo heidelbergensis* has features that seem to combine *Homo erectus, Neandertals,* and *Homo sapiens.*

Most scientists believe that *Homo heidelbergensis* is the last common ancestor shared by Neandertals and modern humans. According to paleoanthropologists, at some point *Homo heidelbergensis* split into two populations. Those living south of the Mediterranean Sea in Africa eventually evolved into *Homo sapiens*, while those living in the caves in Spain and other parts of Europe became Neandertals.

modern humans did. *Homo sapiens neanderthalensis* or *Homo neanderthalensis?* The debate is far from over.

The fossilized bones of Neandertals and their artifacts have been found and studied. They can tell us a lot about who the Neandertals were. But what we'd really like to know is how they behaved. Clearly they were different from modern humans physically. But were they different in the way they lived their lives? The big question is: how human were they? Once again, researchers find that the bones tell very different stories.

Neandertal researchers all agree that the old cartoon description of Neandertal man as a dumb brute who could do little more than club a defenseless animal over the head or drag his mate into a cave by her hair is completely wrong. But the sensitive rituals that formed his image in the 1960s, inspired by the Shanidar excavation, may not be completely accurate either. In the last two decades, much research has focused on Neandertal behavior, which has been mostly misunderstood since Neandertal study began. A big part of the problem has been that researchers have only bones and artifacts to go on. Unfortunately, thoughts and ideas don't fossilize. A lot can be learned about the behavior of a people by studying the tools and other items they used. But once again, much is left up to various researchers' interpretations of the artifacts. Were the Neandertals in any way like us? Were they capable of what is called symbolic thought? Could they plan ahead? Did they work together when they hunted? Did they make art? Did they mourn their dead? Could they even speak to one another? In short, could they do any of the things we think of as human? Only fossils are left to speak for the Neandertals, and the fossils tell different stories depending on how you read them.

It was once thought that Neandertals did not use tools, but evidence of wood spears with stone tips has since been found. Here M. Jegou, a French illustrator specializing in prehistoric topics, offers his vision of what a Neandertal hunting party might have looked like.

FAMILY LIFE

Most paleoanthropologists agree that Neandertals lived in small, extended family groups of men, women, and children. They can tell this by the modest size of rock shelters where Neandertal remains are found and that all three types of skeletons are usually found together. One controversial theory, however, claims that Neandertal men lived separately from the women and children. The scientist who proposed this theory studied a Neandertal site and concluded that the men and women led very different lives, ate different food, and lived in different places. He thinks that Neandertal men selfishly hunted for themselves and didn't share the meat with women and children, who lived in separate camps and gathered food and hunted small animals for themselves. To accept this theory, you would have to imagine that Neandertal males felt so little for their mothers that when they left them they never cared for them again.

Most anthropologists disagree with this theory based on their reading of Neandertal sites. For example, if Neandertal men lived separately from women and children, why are they found buried together?

NEANDERTAL HOMES

Neandertal groups lived in camps in rock shelters. The shelters provided some protection from cold and predators. It appears that Neandertals also built structures resembling tepees out of wood, mammoth bones, and animal skins. In 1996 researchers discovered a four-walled structure built by Neandertals out of rock deep within a cave in southern France.

Floors of caves used by Neandertals are composed of layer upon layer of ash, so it's obvious that Neandertals had fire. In fact, Neandertals are the first human group known to have used fire. They began using fire at least two hundred thousand years ago, the date of the oldest known hearth. Neandertals built simple hearths like campfires. They more than likely used fire for warmth as well as to cook food, making them one of the first human groups to decide how they ate their food. They even may have used fire to smoke fish. Early modern humans built rock-lined hearths that were better than the simple Neandertal fireplaces at capturing and directing the heat of fires.

To survive the cold climates in which they often lived, Neandertals must have worn skins for warmth. Their skin clothes were probably not sewed. Researchers have found no bone needles or other tools for stitching at Neandertal camps. In extended periods

This illustration shows Neandertals in a cave. Neandertals were the first human group to have used fire.

of severe cold, Neandertals probably moved south to warmer climates. Still, it appears that the cold periods when glaciers advanced took their toll on Neandertal populations. DNA studies show little genetic difference in all the Neandertal fossils studied. This indicates that at times throughout their history, Neandertal populations were reduced to a small number of individuals who were able to breed and pass on their genes.

SKILLED HUNTERS

For many years, researchers assumed that Neandertals were not smart enough to coordinate hunting parties to attack large prey. The consensus was they were capable of hunting only individually for small animals or scavenging animals that were already dead.

But most modern anthropologists think that Neandertals were skilled hunters who worked together to kill animals as large as rhinoceroses. Researchers base this theory on several things. First, the bones of large animals with spear tips embedded in them have been found at Neandertal camps. The animals were obviously killed, not scavenged. Second, the skeletons of most Neandertal men have at least one healed fracture, if not several. This suggests that Neandertals probably hunted large animals up close, stabbing them with heavy spears. And last, chemical analysis of Neandertal bones in the last few years can tell us what kinds of foods they ate. The analyses show that European Neandertals ate a great deal of meat, probably more than they would have been able to get from small animals or scavenging.

Studies of Neandertal skeletons also show that sometimes they didn't get enough to eat or enough of the right kinds of vitamins and minerals to stay healthy. For example, examination of the teeth of some Neandertal children shows that at times the enamel

An artist shows a group of Neandertals hunting ancient wild goats known as ibex.

didn't form properly. This condition can be caused by malnutrition. From this information, scientists deduce that Neandertals didn't have the ability to plan ahead for their food needs. They may have relied on the food sources close to their camps rather than following food around. They may not have taken advantage of seasonal fish runs or animal migrations that would have provided a reliable food source. Instead, they just headed out on a hunt when they got hungry, hoping to run into food.

Chemical analyses of fossilized bones also hint at another kind of meat eating: cannibalism. In 1999 researchers studying bones that had been excavated one hundred years ago in modern-day Croatia found that Neandertal skulls and limbs had been broken apart, apparently to remove the brains and marrow. The bones had been cut, not gnawed on, so the damage was the work of people, not animals. Neandertal bones discovered more recently in northern Spain bear the same marks. Some researchers think Neandertals may have eaten their dead in times of hunger for survival. Others see this evidence as a sign of ritualistic behavior. If Neandertals dismembered corpses as part of a burial ritual, it would prove that the bodies held symbolic meaning for the group. The capacity for symbolic thought, by which symbols or images in a person's mind are used to represent objects, persons, and events that are not present, is one important marker that people use to separate humans from prehumans. This mental ability eventually led to sophisticated language, art, and mathematics.

BURIALS

Another important marker of the "humanness" of a group is whether they buried their dead, particularly with some sort of ritual. Ritual burial indicates that the group had some sort of religion or belief in an afterlife. Ever since the Shanidar studies, scientists have been debating whether Neandertals treated their dead with special care. Some scientists maintain that Neandertals buried their dead simply as a way to dispose of them so that they didn't smell and attract predators. Burials, they say, were not for symbolic reasons.

Others see clear evidence of intentional burial beginning at least two hundred thousand years ago with Neandertals. They point to the position in which Neandertal skeletons are found. They were often placed in a sleeping or fetal position. Small groups of skeletons have been found buried together, arranged as though they were holding onto one another or cradling an infant. These scientists believe that flower pollen, red pigment, and tools sometimes found with skeletons did not arrive by chance but were placed with bodies to accompany them into an afterlife.

Recently, new evidence from studies of *Homo heidelbergensis*, Neandertals' ancestor, has supported this view. It appears that *Homo heidelbergensis* were more advanced than previously thought. Researchers have evidence of what they believe to be a burial of *Homo heidelbergensis* forty thousand years ago. This would be the earliest record by far of an intentional burial. If their ancestors buried their dead, surely Neandertals did too.

ART

Art is another activity that is seen as unique to humans. Neandertals left very few pieces of art behind. What they did leave was pretty feeble, leaving some researchers to question whether

Chauvet Cave

At the same time that Neandertals were making primitive pieces of art, such as the flute, early modern humans were carving beautiful bone ornaments and skillfully painting caves. But no one knew how skilled they were until three French cavers in 1994 happened upon a cave in southern France whose walls were covered with breathtaking portraits of animals. The art turned out to be thirty thousand years old, the oldest paintings known in the world. Early modern humans living when the Neandertals were alive left masterful paintings, while Neandertals left almost nothing.

A visitor looks at a flute made from a bear's bone at the archaeological museum in Slovenia. In 1996 archaeologists found the musical instrument, which was made by Neandertals.

it is art at all. The carved and polished ivory tooth from a baby mammoth found by archaeologists in Hungary more than forty years ago was initially thought to have been the work of modern humans. It was later dated to eighty thousand to one hundred thousand years old, before modern humans had arrived and only Neandertals were living in Europe. Recently, researchers found a carved bone at a Neandertal site that may have been worn around the neck as a pendant. Also found in France with other artifacts typical of Neandertals was a piece of flint that was shaped to look like a face. In 1996 archaeologists working in a cave in Slovenia found a flute made from the leg bone of a cave bear. The flute is at least forty thousand years old and the oldest known musical instrument. It may be evidence that Neandertals had music. Other finds at Neandertal sites include rocks and bones with scratches and faint patterns on them, as well as dozens of pieces of manganese dioxide sharpened like black crayons. Neandertals could have used these to decorate animal skins or themselves.

Some scientists suspect that Neandertals didn't make any of these items themselves. They think Neandertals got them from modern humans, who were creating beautiful works of art during that period. Or if they did make them, they were merely copying modern humans, and so the items didn't have any symbolic meaning for them.

But others think that these items prove that Neandertals had some ability to create art and think symbolically. And though only a few art items belonging to Neandertals have been found, that does not mean that Neandertals lacked creativity. Some art forms can't be buried and then dug up tens of thousands of years later. Neandertals may have put their creative energy into dance. Or they may have carved images in wood, which usually decomposes.

TOOLS

The tools Neandertals used and how they made them offer more clues to how their minds worked. We know that Neandertals were highly skilled toolmakers who made lots of different types of tools, all much more sophisticated that the primitive club Marcellin Boule imagined them using. Around two hundred thousand years ago, Neandertals began making stone tools known as Mousterian tools. They made large spearpoints and knives, as well as smaller tools for cutting meat, stripping flesh from animals, scraping hides, and working wood. At first glance, Mousterian tools look like sharp flakes of stone casually broken off a larger rock. But researchers who have tried to make similar tools say that it takes a lot of planning, skill, and brainpower to do it. First, the toolmaker would have to find just the right piece of stone to work with. Next, he would carefully trim the rock to create a rock "core." He would then carefully study the core, finding just the right spots to strike it to release "flakes" that could be used for knives or spearpoints. He would have to know exactly how hard and at what angle to strike the core to produce a usable flake. Researchers who have tried this say it can take months—or even years—to master.

Neandertals were also the first people to haft, or attach, stone points on the ends of wooden spears to create hunting

Found with Neandertal skeletons, these rocks appear to be broken fragments. Closer examination shows they have actually been carefully carved for use as spearheads or tools.

Tool Terminology

The Paleolithic period, also known as the Old Stone Age, ranged from the beginning of the earliest chipped tools, about 750,000 years ago, to the end of the last glaciation, about 15,000 years ago. The period is divided into Lower Paleolithic, Middle Paleolithic, and Upper Paleolithic stages. Modern humans evolved and migrated out of Africa during the Middle Paleolithic. Until around 40,000 years ago, the lifestyle of humans changed very little. Then, relatively suddenly, they began to invent new tools, practice rituals, and create art. This blossoming of culture marks the shift to the Upper Paleolithic, which dates to between 40,000 and 10,000 years ago.

Mousterian is a type of stone tool made during the Middle Paleolithic and associated with early modern humans in the Middle East and Neandertals in the Middle East and Europe.

Aurignacian are more advanced tools and art objects associated with modern humans in the Upper Paleolithic.

Châtelperronian tools appear to be a transition from Mousterian to Aurignacian and are associated with Neandertals during the Upper Paleolithic.

weapons. Some scientists think Neandertals must have had some form of language to pass on this toolmaking technique from generation to generation.

Until the end of the 1970s, scientists believed that the only type of tools European Neandertals made were Mousterian. They believed that the more advanced tool style of the time, called Aurignacian, was carried out by modern humans. Then, in 1980, Neandertal fossils were found with a new type of tool. These were called Châtelperronian for the place in France where they were found. These tools seemed to combine Mousterian and Aurignacian styles.

Neandertals made hunting weapons by attaching their triangular spear points to a handle or shaft. This one is decorated with a carved head.

Most scientists suggested that this was evidence that modern humans had entered Neandertal territory in Europe. They thought that the Neandertals could have borrowed or stolen the tools from their new neighbors.

Then, in 1996, archaeologists found more Châtelperronian blades, body ornaments, and bone tools, as well as the remains of hearths and huts. Skeletons at the site were eventually identified as Neandertals. Most scientists said that it was possible that Neandertals made these tools, but they were copying items used by their new neighbors, modern humans. They were merely imitating, not inventing.

A few scientists disagree, however. After studying the artifacts, they concluded that the Châtelperronian tools were made using older, very different methods than those used by modern humans to create Aurignacian tools. New tests have indicated that the Châtelperronian tools were much older than previously thought. If these tests are accurate (unfortunately, dating fossils and artifacts is not an exact science), Neandertals were making Châtelperronian tools long before modern humans established themselves in Europe. That would mean that Neandertals were inventing more advanced tools, not imitating, and may have been capable of symbolic thought. Neandertals would need to think symbolically to envision how the tool would look when finished, and then plan how to make it happen.

About forty thousand years ago, after tens of thousands of years with little change in behavior, Neandertals seemed to suddenly blossom. They began using more complex tools and even art objects and building better dwellings and hearths. At the same time, new people moved into Europe. They came armed with new and better inventions and ways of doing things. What happened when those two groups of people met is a mystery that scientists are trying to solve.

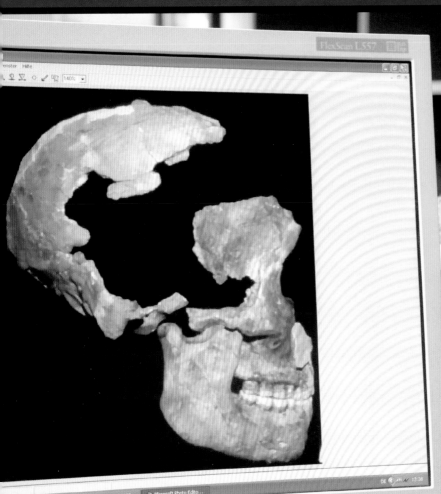

THE HUMAN FOSSIL RECORD

VOLUME ONE

*Terminology
and Craniodental
Morphology
of Genus* Homo
(Europe)

CHAPTER SEVEN
WHAT HAPPENED? THE MYSTERY OF NEANDERTAL DISAPPEARANCE

Most researchers agree that Neandertals were brave hunters and skilled toolmakers. They built dwellings, used fire, cared for their sick and injured, and communicated with one another in some way. They buried their dead, perhaps with the notion of an afterlife. They were much stronger and better adapted physically to cold climates than the strange new people arriving from the south. They flourished for thousands of generations. So why, a little more than ten thousand years after modern humans settled in Europe, did Neandertals disappear?

Scientists divide into two general camps when answering that question. The majority camp says that Neandertals were completely replaced by modern humans who had spread to Europe from their birthplace in Africa. The two groups looked and behaved so differently that they must have been separate species that wouldn't—or couldn't—have children together. The Neandertals slowly lost out to the newcomers, and the Neandertals went extinct. The scientists who promote this theory offer several reasons to explain Neandertal extinction. First is that modern humans may have directly killed off Neandertals through violence. Or they may have carried some new disease that was deadly to Neandertals. Another theory is that modern humans were simply smarter and more skilled than Neandertals

A German scientist studies a Neandertal skull to try to find more information on Neandertals' place in the human fossil record.

and better at getting food, leaving less food for Neandertals, who eventually died out.

Other scientists in the majority camp think that the climate may have done in the Neandertals. Neandertals disappeared as Europe was entering the last ice age. As the cold became more extreme, many of the plants and animals that Neandertals depended on vanished. Neandertals headed south for warmer temperatures. But as their habitat (home territory) shrank, so did their populations until none were left.

Many scientists think a combination of competition and climate destroyed the Neandertals. Neandertals had successfully weathered cold spells before. Although they may have lost population during times of severe cold, enough of them survived for the group to bounce back. But this time, they were facing severe cold and competition from their new neighbors. The combination of the two may have proved to be too much for the Neandertals. As Neandertals retreated to warmer refuges, they may have found that modern humans were already there. Although Neandertals were accustomed to the cold and better suited physically for it, modern humans had better ways of dealing with the cold. They may have built superior shelters and hearths, wore warmer clothes, and traded with other modern human groups for food and tools.

The minority camp believes that the two groups would have recognized each other as fellow humans. In the thousands of years that they lived side by side, the Neandertals and modern humans would have exchanged tools, ideas, and genes as they had families together. There were fewer Neandertals, though, so after thousands of years of interbreeding, the genes responsible for the classic Neandertal features faded away. According to this camp, Neandertals didn't go extinct in the classic sense of the word—they were absorbed into the *Homo sapiens* population.

GENETIC STUDIES

Members of the extinction, or replacement, camp say the proof is in the genes.

How do you tell whether Neandertals had children with early modern humans and are among our ancestors? One of the best ways is to look at their DNA. DNA in our cells tells who our ancestors were, but it eventually deteriorates after death. In most cases, all of it is gone from fossils after fifty thousand to one hundred thousand years. In 1997 researchers sacrificed a piece of bone from the original Neander Valley skeleton. They ground it up and were able to recover a tiny snippet of mitochondrial DNA. They compared the Neander skeleton's DNA to present-day human populations. They found that Neandertal DNA didn't look anything like our DNA. If Neandertal and modern human DNA are very different, then they must be different species that couldn't have children together.

Some scientists say that the DNA test settles the matter. But others say the field of genetic study is too new and has problems. Even an expert who worked on the Neander skeleton DNA study says that the data do not show positive evidence of interbreeding, but that doesn't mean that interbreeding definitely didn't take place.

According to scientists who think that Neandertals and early modern humans did interbreed, the bones tell a different story than the DNA.

Problems with DNA Studies

Studying human DNA, especially from fossils, is tricky. First, it's hard to get DNA from ancient bones. When an organism dies, bacteria and fungi attack its tissues. Much of the DNA is destroyed, and the little bit remaining is broken into short pieces. If a scientist does manage to recover a tiny amount, it's usually contaminated by bacteria and fungi and even from scientists who have handled the bones. Any flake of skin or piece of hair from someone who has come in contact with the skeleton can throw off the DNA test results. The scientist in the lab may think she has found evidence of modern human DNA in an ancient bone, but really she's detected a flake of skin from the archaeologist who excavated the skeleton or a stray hair from a museum worker who handled the bone.

Another problem is that early modern human DNA is hard to study. The reason is that the DNA from an early modern human fossil and the DNA of a lab worker is so similar, it's virtually impossible to tell them apart. Therefore, the samples can easily be contaminated by the lab worker's DNA. It is easier for scientists to compare Neandertal DNA to present-day humans. Because Neandertal DNA is so different from our own, contamination by DNA from modern people working with the bones can be identified easier and the results thrown out. DNA testing has determined that there is no Neandertal DNA in modern people. But the tests have not been able to help much with finding out about the early modern humans that Neandertals may have been in contact with.

Researchers say that more and better DNA samples from Neandertals could tell what color hair and eyes Neandertals had, what genetic diseases they suffered from, and possibly even if they were able to talk.

HYBRID SKELETONS

Throughout the years, archaeologists have found skeletons of early modern humans that seem to have a few Neandertal traits. Scientists in the minority camp have taken that as evidence of interbreeding between the two groups. Scientists in the replacement camp say that a few modern humans and Neandertals might have had children together, but not enough to make a difference, and that these "hybrid" children would not have been able to have children of their own.

Then, in 1998, archaeologists in Portugal unearthed the skeleton of a young child buried nearly twenty-five thousand years ago. Erik Trinkaus, professor of anthropology at

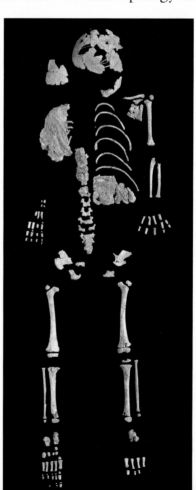

This skeleton of a young child was found in Portugal in 1998. The researcher who studied the bones thinks they may represent a hybrid of modern human and Neandertal.

Washington University, studied the bones. At first he thought it was an early modern child with a stocky build, because Neandertals were supposed to have disappeared from the area about three thousand years earlier. But what he found was an early modern child with a lot of Neandertal features in addition to the stocky build. The child's chin and teeth look like a modern human's, but the jaw and short, thick body look more like a Neandertal's. The short lower limbs were notable. Neandertals are identified by their unusually short lower legs, but early modern humans in Europe had long, slender legs. This is evidence, say Trinkaus and others, that Neandertals didn't simply become extinct. For Neandertal features to be present in a modern human child thousands of years after Neandertals disappeared, significant interbreeding must have occurred between the two populations, at least in that part of the world, and Neandertals became part of our modern human family. No, say other scientists, it's simply a stocky modern human child.

In 2003 another skeleton was found in a cave complex in northwestern Romania. It's considered to be the earliest *Homo sapiens* fossil found in Europe, yet it has some distinct Neandertal features. So do the thirty-one-thousand-year-old modern human fossils found in caves in the Czech Republic in 2007. And the last Neandertals living in Croatia look more modern than do most other Neandertals. According to a few scientists, Neandertal features, including stocky builds, large noses, and occipital buns, are even present in modern Europeans.

So did early modern humans in Europe push Neandertals to extinction, or do modern Europeans harbor a tiny bit of Neandertal in their genes? The debate is far from over.

Overlap

Neandertals may have seen their first modern humans in modern Israel ninety thousand years ago or perhaps more. The newcomers would have looked taller and slimmer, with smaller faces that had high foreheads and slight browridges. Their skin may have been darker as a result of evolving in the warm climate of Africa. To Neandertals, modern humans may have looked too delicate to survive the harsh climate they were used to. The two groups may have had differences in appearance, but they lived very similar lives. They made stone tools, lived in rock shelters, and used fire.

Modern humans, however, did survive and continued to push into Neandertal territory in Europe starting between forty-three thousand and forty-six thousand years ago. Fossil remains suggest that as modern humans spread, Neandertals retreated. Until recently, it appeared that the last holdout for Neandertals was in eastern Europe, where they died out about thirty thousand years ago. In 2006 researchers found tools known only to be used by Neandertals in a cave in Gibraltar. The tools date to twenty-eight thousand years ago. That means that Neandertals survived at least two thousand years longer than previously thought.

According to these dates, Neandertals and modern humans both lived in Europe for ten thousand to twelve thousand years before Neandertals disappeared from the fossil record. And they overlapped in the Middle East possibly as long as sixty thousand years. Whether they lived close enough to each other to interact regularly or saw each other only in passing is harder to tell. Some scientists say that the land was so big and the people so few that the two groups would have had little chance to meet. Clearly, though, there was plenty of time for them to do so.

Regardless of what camp you're in, however, Neandertals disappeared from the fossil record around twenty-eight thousand years ago and *Homo sapiens* became the sole remaining human species, surviving, thriving, and pushing to almost every corner of the world. Early modern humans must have had some very important advantage over Neandertals. What was it?

CULTURAL REVOLUTION

Scientists note that between forty thousand and fifty thousand years ago, the same time they began spreading into Europe, *Homo sapiens* became, well, smarter. Neandertals and *Homo sapiens* had both lived in the Middle East for tens of thousands of years without one group seeming more advanced than the other. They both made Mousterian tools. Then modern humans suddenly began making fancier tools out of bones and antlers as well as stone. They also began carving animal figurines and wearing beads and pendants. Scientists aren't sure what brought on these changes. It might be that modern humans' brains changed through an evolutionary process called mutation. As a result, early modern humans were able to remember and organize information in their heads better than they had been able to before. This process led to better toolmaking, long-range planning for hunting, symbolic thought expressed in artwork, and perhaps the most important advantage of all—language. Fully developed language would have allowed early modern humans to share information between groups, organize hunting expeditions, tell stories to create bonds among group members, and develop trading networks. But did only modern humans use language?

NEANDERTAL LANGUAGE

Early scientists who studied the first Neandertal skeletons thought that Neandertals could do little more than grunt to one another. But some modern researchers believe that Neandertals must have had some form of communication to organize hunts, create burial rituals and some artwork, and pass on knowledge of toolmaking.

We humans can talk because we have an organ called a larynx, or voice box. The voice box hangs at the back of the tongue from a small bone called a hyoid bone. It looks a little like a horseshoe. In the 1970s, researchers used a computer to reconstruct what a Neandertal mouth and throat would have looked like based on a Neandertal skull. They decided that the shape of Neandertals' mouths and throats was much different from that of modern humans and that Neandertals would not have been able to make certain sounds and speak as we do. In 1983, however, researchers discovered a hyoid bone from a sixty-thousand-year-old Neandertal. The hyoid bone looked just like that of modern humans. So Neandertals probably had voice boxes similar to ours and therefore were capable of making the same sounds we do.

A few years ago, scientists studied fossilized ear bones from *Homo heidelbergensis*, Neandertals' closest ancestor. From those bones, scientists concluded that *Homo heidelbergensis* could hear the same range of sounds that modern humans do. Because all primates make sounds similar to the ones they hear, *Homo heidelbergensis*—and therefore Neandertals—probably made the same sounds that modern humans did and may have been capable of language. It's impossible to tell from skeletons how complex their language might have been, but some scientists think Neandertals could talk to one another.

Thoroughly Modern Man

Researchers have traditionally believed that *Homo sapiens* began thinking symbolically and making sophisticated art objects and tools relatively recently—about forty thousand to fifty thousand years ago. That would be about the time they were moving into Europe and more than one hundred thousand years after evolving to be anatomically modern. This theory is based mostly on excavations in Europe that seem to show a sudden flowering of art, ritual, technology, and other evidence of modern thinking. But new discoveries in Africa suggest that those changes may have begun much earlier and evolved over a long period. If so, that would mean that *Homo sapiens* were our mental equals by the time they became anatomically

This model of Neandertals in a museum in Mexico City, Mexico, shows Neandertal men making cave paintings.

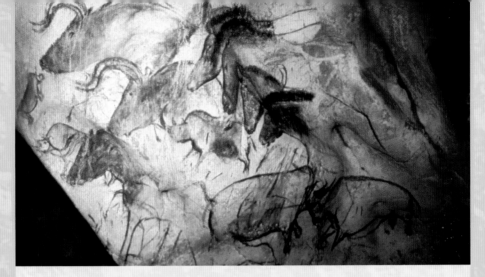

These ancient drawings of animals were found in Chauvet Cave in France in 1994.

modern, if not earlier. It's possible, even, that symbolic thought can be traced all the way back to *Homo heidelbergensis*, the last common ancestor between Neandertals and *Homo sapiens*. That, of course, would be good news for the camp of scientists who argue that Neandertals also were capable of symbolic thought.

Some scientists suggest that Neandertals may have been responsible for the flowering in culture of early modern humans. These scientists point out that within a few thousand years of encountering Neandertals in Europe, early modern humans were making glorious cave paintings and other art. Yet the early modern humans who migrated to Australia, where there were no Neandertals, did none of that. The sudden growth in culture may have been due to increased population and competition. As populations grew and more people had to share resources, our ancestors had to come up with more creative ways to obtain food and materials needed for toolmaking, leading to better technology. They also would have run into other groups of people more often. Our ancestors may have begun to make special tools, wear jewelry, or paint their bodies as a way of identifying which group they belonged to.

Some scientists have another intriguing theory: perhaps the crucial gene that made early modern humans smarter and sparked the artistic revolution actually came from Neandertals through interbreeding.

One expert thinks that Neandertals actually sang to one another. Steven Mithin, a professor of early history at Reading University in Great Britain, believes that Neandertals and other early humans used an early form of communication that evolved into music and language as we know it. This early communication would have helped Neandertals survive the tough conditions they lived in as they sang their babies to sleep, chanted and danced during times of celebration, and mourned their dead with song. This early form of language would have been no match for a fully developed language, though.

EARLY TRADERS

Scientists most often cite language as the advantage that could explain why modern humans triumphed over Neandertals. But another reason is gaining in popularity: trade. Based on the artifacts found at their sites, some scientists see evidence that early modern humans kept in regular contact with other nearby groups of *Homo sapiens.* By doing so, early modern humans were able to share knowledge and hunting grounds and trade for food and the raw goods needed to make tools and other items. So even if modern humans weren't as strong or fast as Neandertals, they used resources more wisely by sharing and trading for them.

Early modern humans may have also been more mobile. Scientists studying Neandertal and modern human sites can tell what animals were eaten and even in what seasons they were killed. Based on this evidence, some researchers conclude that modern humans moved with the seasons and followed animals as they migrated. Neandertals, on the other hand, appear to have stayed put for long periods. If this is true, then modern

Neandertal shelters, such as this one found in 1909 in Peyzac-le-Moustier, France, indicate that Neandertals stayed in one location for long periods of time. (The cave has a preservation structure built around it to protect if for further study.)

humans would have had more variety in their diet, which meant better-rounded intake of vitamins and minerals. This would have led to healthier babies, longer lives, and eventually an increase in population. If Neandertals stuck to one place permanently, they would have eventually run low on food and had to work harder to find more. They would not have been as healthy or lived as long, meaning their populations wouldn't have grown as fast as modern human populations did.

"Rubbish!" says Trinkaus, who doesn't believe that Neandertals were just "sitting around being stupid, waiting to become extinct."[3] He believes that Neandertals were smart enough to move if necessary to find more food.

FIRST RACISTS?

Another interesting and disturbing theory is that Neandertals and modern humans thought about people and things differently. This theory suggests that Neandertals saw people as different from objects and treated all people the same. Early modern humans may have been able to mix the two and see some people not as humans but as objects, to be used or, perhaps, disposed of. So, the advantage modern humans may have had was racism, the idea that one group of people is superior to another. When one group of people views another group as less than human, they are more likely to mistreat the "inferior" group.

EQUAL RIGHTS

Yet another explanation for the Neandertals' demise is their equal treatment of men and women. Recent studies show that Neandertals were just as good at hunting as early modern humans. Lots of healed fractures in the skeletons of both men and women suggest that everyone participated in the hunts. Also, some researchers say there is little evidence that Neandertals collected seeds and other foods or made crafts. If that's true, Neandertal women weren't hanging around home gathering nuts, berries, and other foods and sewing warm clothes as early modern human women were. Instead, judging by the number of fractures in Neandertal women's skeletons, they were out with the men hunting large and dangerous prey. In the process, they were injured and even killed. Early modern human women, in contrast, appear to have stuck closer to home. Instead of going on dangerous hunts, they gathered nuts, berries, and other foods, sewed warm clothes, and took care of the children. It may be that a division of labor allowed early modern human women and children to live longer than their Neandertal counterparts. And more women and children mean a growing population. Other scientists disagree with this theory. They say that Neandertals didn't just hunt big game. They also relied on small game, such as turtles and birds, and men as well as women may have sewed clothes.

Much of Neandertal research and debate focuses on why Neandertals disappeared. All this attention on extinction can lead people to think of Neandertals as failures. What people don't realize is that Neandertals were the dominant species in Europe for hundreds of thousands of years. Modern humans have only been in charge for about forty thousand years. Neandertals were strong, made impressive tools, and took care of one another, managing to survive in some of the harshest environments ever lived in by any human group. That they were our equals in many ways makes their disappearance all the more mysterious.

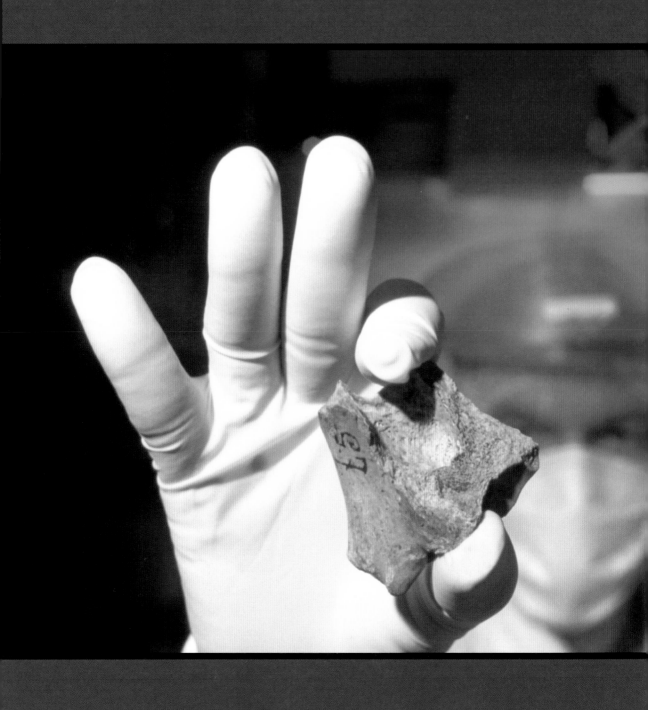

CHAPTER EIGHT
THE FUTURE OF NEANDERTAL RESEARCH

Scientists agree that it's an exciting time to be studying Neandertals. Because we have found more of their skeletons than those of any other ancient human, the latest improvements in dating techniques and new technologies in paleoanthropology are usually tried on Neandertals first.

NEANDERTAL BLUEPRINT

In 2006 two independent teams of scientists announced that they were going to try to sequence the Neandertal genome. This means that scientists plan to map the location of all genes, together known as the genome, of Neandertals. This work would provide what might be considered a blueprint for building a Neandertal. Researchers hope the genome will provide answers to questions such as what color hair and skin Neandertals had, whether they spoke, and if they interbred with early modern humans.

Until recently, it seemed impossible to find enough genetic material to be able to sequence, or rebuild, the Neandertal genome. That's because DNA in old bones breaks down into millions of pieces that were too short to work with. But a new technology allows scientists to string those tiny pieces of DNA together to get a more complete picture—and it allows them to

A technician prepares a sample of bone from a Neandertal fossil for DNA analysis.

Svante Paabo, holding a replica of a Neandertal bone in 1997, leads a research team that is working to map the Neandertal genome.

work about one hundred times faster than they could before.

Neandertals will be the first human group other than us to have their genome mapped. (Scientists finished mapping the genome for *Homo sapiens* in 2003. We probably have between thirty thousand and forty thousand genes.) Neandertals will also be the first extinct species to be mapped. That's an indication of how much interest there is in Neandertals within the scientific community.

Svante Paabo, the leader of one of the research teams, began searching for a Neandertal bone with enough genetic material in it in the mid-1990s. He also needed a bone that hadn't been contaminated with DNA from modern people who had handled it. After testing and discarding seventy bone and tooth samples, Paabo's team finally found a short thigh bone from a Neandertal man, thirty-eight thousand years old. It had been collected in a cave in Croatia. The bone had been tossed in a box of bones and not handled much. As a result, it wasn't contaminated, and it contained enough DNA for Paabo to work with.

The two teams are working with nuclear DNA, the genetic material found in the nucleus of cells. Nuclear DNA contains information from a mother and a father. Previous DNA studies used mitochondrial DNA, which contains information only from the mother. Therefore, the new studies should provide a more complete picture of Neandertals than earlier studies could.

Paabo estimates that Neandertal and modern human genes will be as much as 99.96 percent identical. It may seem as if there is no room for differences between the two groups. But it's the tiny differences in modern human and Neandertal genomes that made all the difference. Somewhere in that 0.04 percent difference, scientists expect to find the genes responsible for allowing *Homo sapiens* to flourish while Neandertals declined. Nobody yet knows precisely what genes make us human and where they are. But scientists will soon be able to compare the Neandertal genome to ours. Any genes that Neandertals don't share with modern humans will help scientists determine what makes Neandertals—and *Homo sapiens*—unique. They're going to look particularly at genes that are involved in language and brain size. When a gene of interest is identified, it can be placed in a mouse to see if it changes the way the mouse acts. That could give scientists a clue to how that gene affected Neandertal behavior. It's the next best thing to having a living Neandertal.

BEYOND DNA STUDIES

In addition to DNA, scientists can study many other molecules and chemical elements found in Neandertal bones and teeth. For example, the elements carbon, nitrogen, strontium, and calcium can be extracted from bones. These four elements come from food and water. By studying them, scientists can gather information about a Neandertal's diet.

Scientists may soon be able to use bone chemical studies to answer the question of how much Neandertals migrated. The specific chemical elements in groundwater vary from region to region. Extracting those elements from Neandertal bones could show how far an individual or group of Neandertals traveled.

These chemicals don't break down as quickly as ancient DNA does. So scientists may be able to use chemical studies to gather information on skeletons that are too old for DNA studies.

VIRTUAL FOSSILS

Human fossils are very fragile and can be damaged during study. Researchers are developing new methods of study that are easier on the bones. Scientists are increasingly using computerized tomography (CT) scanning to study the internal details of Neandertal skeletons. A CT scan uses computerized photography to show the inside of a body without disturbing it from the outside. For example, a CT scan of the inner ear of a Neandertal skull can reveal what range of sound Neandertals heard without researchers having to cut into the skull.

Scientists are also using new computer software to create and study Neandertal skeletons. Scientists can, for example, scan into the computer an incomplete Neandertal skull and then fill in the missing pieces from other skulls to create a complete skull on screen. Scientists can then work with that virtual skull rather than the actual one. Researchers can scan into the computer bones that have been warped and twisted during the fossilization process. Then they can straighten the bones out on-screen, which they can't do with the real ones.

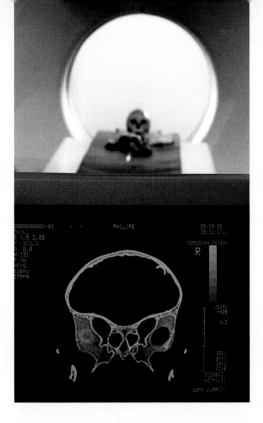

This Neandertal skull is getting a CT scan so researchers can study the inside of the bones without having to cut into them. This skull is from the skeleton of a Neandertal child found in Gibraltar in 1926.

EXCITEMENT AND FRUSTRATION

It's an exciting time for researchers because Neandertal skeletons are popping up all over—in France, southern Italy, eastern Europe, the Iberian Peninsula (Spain and Portugal), and the Middle East. One Neandertal expert remarked that it seems Neandertal remains are everywhere you look.

It's an exciting time for Neandertal researchers but also a frustrating time. After finding the remains of about four hundred Neandertals and hundreds of thousands of their stone tools and artifacts and studying this evidence for generations, there are still huge disagreements over what it all means. These debates are infamous in the scientific community for how heated they can be. Why the lack of agreement? For one thing, archaeology is not an exact science.

AN INEXACT SCIENCE

The technologies used to study Neandertals are not perfect and can cause problems. For example, the age of fossil skeletons and artifacts is crucial to answering many questions about ancient people. Scientists use these dates to develop theories about when and where Neandertals evolved, what tools they used, how long they overlapped with early modern humans, when they disappeared, and other things. But the techniques provide just a range of dates, and they aren't always accurate. When new technologies provide new dates, researchers must revise or even discard their old theories.

As we've seen, studies of ancient DNA aren't perfect either. For the tests to be more reliable, scientists say they need many more samples from Neandertals and early modern humans and the samples have to be free of contamination. But ancient DNA is hard to come by, and you have to grind up bones to get it. Is it worth it?

Archaeology is not an exact science because no matter how many Neandertal camps, tools, and skeletons are found, there will always be different ways to interpret the fossils. Neandertals have been plagued by researchers who use the evidence to further their own ideas about human evolution—a practice that is still happening. One scientist has said that there are two kinds of people—those who think Neandertals are dumb and those who think Neandertals are smart. The scientist was exaggerating to make a point about Neandertal study. But there is quite a polarization in the field between scientists who think Neandertals were the equals of modern humans and were absorbed into our family and the majority of researchers who think that Neandertals were an inferior subspecies who went extinct.

When scientists look at evidence, what they see often depends on what they're looking for. The same piece of ancient bone or stone tool can mean very different things to two equally qualified experts, depending on whether they're looking for evidence that Neandertals were a different species or not. For example, one researcher might look at a Neandertal tool made from local rock and see evidence of Neandertals' intelligent use of local resources. Another researcher may look at the same tool and conclude that Neandertals weren't advanced enough to plan into the future and travel long distances to gather a certain rock for toolmaking, as modern humans did.

Scientists will always be tempted to bring their biases with them when they study new evidence. It is human nature to do so. We interpret new information based on what we already know and think about the subject and its place in the world. That doesn't mean that the conclusions we draw are wrong. Remember Marcellin Boule? Although his goals and tactics weren't always admirable when studying the Old Man of La Chapelle, his larger conclusions were correct. Modern scientists agree that human evolution was treelike, not linear, just as Boule said. And most Neandertal researchers agree with Boule that Neandertals were not our ancestors but rather a side branch on that tree that went extinct.

A BUM RAP

Some scientists worry that despite new evidence and new attitudes, Neandertals are still getting a bum rap. These scientists are concerned that even when evidence points to higher symbolic thought among Neandertals (such as burial with grave goods, ritualistic cannibalism, and pieces of artwork), it's quickly explained away. Some will say the tools and pollen must have washed in accidentally or Neandertals are barbarians and must have stolen them from modern humans.

The Dating Game

Our understanding of human evolution depends on the ability to accurately date ancient skeletons and the artifacts found with them. Scientists look at three things to tell how old a skeleton is: the location of the body, the items found near the body, and the bones themselves.

In the early days of paleoanthropology, scientists relied on relative dating. This means that they ordered fossils from oldest to youngest. Because of the way sedimentary rocks form, lower layers are older than higher layers, making it possible to determine which fossils found in those layers are oldest and which are youngest. Relative dating can be useful, but by itself, it cannot assign any absolute age to fossils. Modern researchers are more likely to analyze soil and rock samples surrounding the bones for more accurate clues to the skeleton's age.

Scientists also study the objects found on and near the skeleton. The types of tools, art objects, and animal bones can tell a lot about the age of the skeleton. This method can be misleading, though. For example, researchers have mistakenly identified Neandertal skeletons as early modern humans because they were found with tools that experts at the time thought were used only by early modern humans.

Scientists also investigate the bones themselves using radiometric dating. The basis of this dating technique is that certain elements change from one form to another over time at known rates. One way to determine the age of an ancient bone (or any other once-living material) is by measuring how much a radioactive form of carbon (carbon 14) it contains. Carbon 14 decays at a predictable rate. Measuring how much carbon 14 a bone still contains gives scientists a good estimate of its age. But radiocarbon dating is most accurate on material younger than forty thousand years old. Radiocarbon dating can produce inaccurate results for bones older than that. Carbon dating works well on organic material such as shell, wood, bone, and teeth.

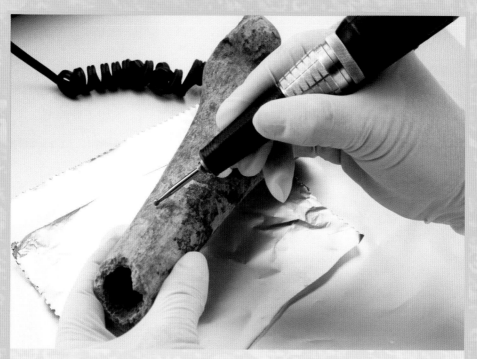

A sample is being taken from this bone so that it can be carbon dated.

Another technique measures the potassium and argon found in a sample instead of carbon. As radioactive potassium decays, it turns into argon. The more argon in a sample, the older it is because the potassium has had more time to change. The more potassium a sample contains, the younger it is. But this method works best for materials older than half a million years. So neither of these methods is ideal for most ancient human bones.

Newer techniques include electron spin resonance and thermoluminescence (or heat light). Scientists use these techniques to measure time by observing how exposure to heat or light has affected material found near a skeleton. These methods have the potential to be much more accurate, but they are still new and have some bugs to be worked out.

On the other hand, other scientists are concerned that scientists who assign human attributes to Neandertals are being overly sentimental, as if they are trying to make up for all those years that Neandertals were mischaracterized as stooping beasts. Though we've moved away from Boule's version of Neandertals, many people, including some experts, seem uncomfortable with the idea of Neandertals as our equals. We, unfortunately, are used to insects, birds, and animals going extinct, but not humans. Our closest relatives going extinct can be upsetting. It's easier to accept if we believe that Neandertals were inferior, somehow less suited for survival. But the thought that people who were the equals of early modern humans went extinct can be frightening. If Neandertals went extinct after more than two hundred thousand years of surviving in a challenging world, who's to say that *Homo sapiens*, who have been around half that time, won't meet the same fate eventually? And if Neandertals were just like us, what makes us unique?

A big part of what makes the debate about Neandertals so sensitive is what it reveals about us. We coexisted in Europe for ten thousand years or more with another species or subspecies. How did we treat those other people? It's quite likely that we caused them to go extinct, either on purpose or by accident. What if we, modern humans, did intentionally kill off another human species? What if the evolutionary advantage that we had was racism—the capability to divide people into "us" and "others" and then treat the "others" as less human? That's not something we want to hear about ourselves. It's much nicer to think that we accidentally wiped out Neandertals by being smarter and better adapted. Or that we didn't kill them off at all but rather welcomed them into our families. But, as Milford H. Wolpoff, professor of anthropology at the University of Michigan, says, to fully understand ourselves, we need to know what our ancestors were like. So scientists will continue to study early modern humans and Neandertals and come up with theories about how they lived and died. And some of those theories will be upsetting or unpleasant, leading to emotional debate.

According to some scientists, what the field of Neandertal research most needs is a change in attitude. It may be time to stop trying to understand Neandertals by comparing them to us. Instead of judging them by our standards of what it means to be human, it would be better to focus on Neandertals as unique people living in a different world and dealing with it in their own way. They may have been different from us, but that doesn't mean they were less human. In fact, one Neandertal and early modern human expert recently said that a careful study of human evolution as a whole shows that modern humans, not Neandertals, are the strange ones. Modern humans are the only hominids that lack browridges and have small faces, reduced naval cavities, and other unique features. To better understand human evolution, he says, we should not be asking how Neandertals are different from us, but why modern humans are so unusual.

As our closest relatives and the last human species we shared the world with, we will always be fascinated with Neandertals. And perhaps it's "human" nature to be most interested in comparing them to us, to use Neandertals to better understand ourselves. So researchers will continue to look for clues to who the Neandertals were, how they lived, and why they disappeared. And we'll continue to wonder about how human they were. Were they curious about the world and their place in it? Did they tell stories about the past? Did they dream about the future? Did they think and feel as we do? That's something the bones will never be able to tell us.

artifacts: objects that are made or modified by humans

common ancestor: the most recent ancestral form or species from which two different species evolved

Cro-Magnons: an early group of *Homo sapiens* that lived about 40,000 years ago in present-day Europe

DNA: short for deoxyribonucleic acid, it is the molecule that carries genetic information from parent to offspring

evolution: the process of change by which new species develop from existing species over time

extinction: the disappearance of a species or population

fossil: the physical remains of plants or animals preserved in rock, petrified bones, or wood

gene: a segment of DNA that carries information on hereditary characteristics, such as height, hair color, or susceptibility to a certain disease

genome: the full set of DNA in a cell or an organism

glaciation: the formation of large sheets of ice across the land, marking the beginning of an ice age

hominid: all members of the human family tree, from the point when the human line split from the apes

Homo erectus: a species of hominid that lived between 1.8 million years ago and 300,000 years ago and was the first *Homo* species to migrate beyond Africa

Homo neanderthalensis: a species of hominid that lived between about 200,000 and 30,000 years ago in Europe and western Asia. It may be a subspecies of *Homo sapiens* but is generally accepted to be a distinct species.

Homo sapiens sapiens: modern humans, who evolved to their present form about 100,000 years ago

mitochondrial DNA: DNA found in the mitochondria, a small round body found in most cells. It is passed to offspring from mothers, but not fathers.

mutation: change in genetic material that results from an error when DNA divides. Mutations can be harmful, beneficial, or neither.

natural selection: a process by which the forms of an organism in a population best adapted to the local environment survive and pass on their traits to subsequent generations. Less well-adapted forms die out, thus ridding the population of their genetic traits.

paleoanthropology: the study of the human fossil record

species: a set of all individuals—either plants or animals—that can mate and produce fertile offspring

SOURCE NOTES

9 James Shreeve, *The Neandertal Enigma*, New York:Avon Books, 1995, 26.

31 H. G. Wells, "The Grisly Folk," *Storyteller Magazine*, April 1921, http://www.trussel.com/prehist/grisly.htm (September 7, 2007).

88 Trinkaus, Erik. "Trade or Die." *Foreign Policy*, Jul/Aug 2005, 21.

SELECTED BIBLIOGRAPHY

Adler, Jerry. "Cavemen, Chimps and Us." *Newsweek*, July 31, 2006, 48.

———. "Who Gave Us Our Smarts?" *Newsweek*, November 27, 2006, 13.

Alper, Joe. "Rethinking Neanderthals." *Smithsonian*, June 2003, 83–87.

Allman, William F. "Dawn of Creativity." *US News and World Report*, May 20, 1996, 52–58.

Archaeology. "Neanderthals on the Hunt." March/April 2007, 15.

Arsuaga, Juan Luis. "Requiem for a Heavyweight." *Natural History*, December 2002/January 2003, 43–48.

Avasthi, Amitabh. "Oldest Europeans Were Swingers." *Science Now*, May 18, 2005, 2–3.

Bailey, Shara E., and Jean-Jacques Hublin. "Dental Remains from the Grotte du Renne at Arcy-sur-Cure." *Journal of Human Evolution*, May 2006, 485–508.

Binns, Corey. "But Did They Do It?" *Natural History*, February 2007, 14.

Brainard, Jeffrey. "Giving Neandertals Their Due: Similarities with Modern Humans Shift the Image of the Caveman Brute." *Science News*, August 1, 1998, 72–75.

Bower, Bruce. "Fossil May Expose Humanity's Hybrid Roots." *Science News*, March 20, 1999, 295.

———. "French Site Sparks Neandertal Debate." *Science News*, September 17, 2005, 189.

———. "Gene Test Probes Neandertal Origins." *Science News*, July 8, 2000, 21.

———. "In the Neandertal Mind." *Science News*, September 18, 2004, 183–184.

———. "Neandertals Show Staying Power in Europe." *Science News*, October 30, 1999, 277.

———. "Neandertals' Tough Stone Age Lives." *Science News*, December 16, 2006, 398.

———. "Noses Didn't Need Cold to Evolve." *Science News*, April 23, 2005, 270.

———. "Skull Canals Spark Speech-Origin Dispute." *Science News*, February 20, 1999, 118.

———. "Stone Age Cutups." *Science News*, April 16, 2005, 244.

———. "Stone Age Role Revolution." *Science News*, December 12, 2006, 358.

Casselman, Anne. "Will We Ever Clone a Caveman?" *Discover*, September 2006, 20.

Economist. "Cracking the Neanderthal Code." November 18, 2006, 83–84.

———. "The Neanderthal Genome Project: A Study with a Lot of Balls." July 29, 2006, 72–73.

Foreign Policy. "Trade or Die." July/August 2005, 21.

Fullagar, Richard, and Georgina Hickey. "Neanderthal Face?" *Nature Australia*, Summer 2004, 15.

Gore, Rick. "The Dawn of Humans: Neandertals." *National Geographic*, January 1996, 2–35.

Gould, Stephen J. "Evolution as Fact and Theory." *Discover*, May 1981. March 26, 2007. http://www.talkorigins.org/faqs/evolution-fact.html (August 2, 2007).

Guatelli-Steinberg, Debbie, et al. "Anterior Tooth Growth Periods in Neandertals Were Comparable to Those of Modern Humans." *Proceedings of the National Academy of Sciences of the United States of America*, October 4, 2005, 14,197–14,202.

Highham, Tom, et al. "Revised Direct Radiocarbon Dating of the Vindija G1 Upper Paleolithic Neandertals." *Proceedings of the National Academy of Sciences of the United States of America*, January 17, 2006, 553–557.

Horan, Richard D., et al. "How Trade Saved Humanity from Biological Exclusion: An Economic Theory of Neanderthal Extinction." *Journal of Economic Behavior & Organization*, September 2005, 1–29.

Hublin, Jean-Jacques. "Brothers or Cousins?" *Archaeology*, September/October 2000, 49–54.

———. "The New Neandertal." *Archaeology*, July/August 2005, 61–66.

Hublin, Jean-Jacques, and Svante Paabo, "Neandertals." *Current Biology*, February 2006, 113–114.

Jordan, Paul. *Neanderthal: Neanderthal Man and the Story of Human Origins.* Somerset, UK: Sutton Publishing, 1999.

Joyce, Christopher. "Neanderthals Found to Live in More Recent Past." *All Things Considered*. Minnesota Public Radio. September 13, 2006.

Kahn, Chris. "Study: Neanderthals Grew Up Much Faster than Modern Humans." *Grand Forks Herald*, April 29, 2004, 6B.

Klein, Richard G. "Was the Culprit Climate or Culture?" *Science*, July 2, 2004, 45.

La Pierre, Yvette. "The Mystery of the Neandertals." *Muse*, September 2001, 8–17.

Lemonick, Michael D., and Andrea Dorfman. "The 160,000-Year-Old Man." *Time*, June 23, 2003, 56–58.

Lemonick, Michael. "Nowhere Men: Scientists Debate What Happened to the Neandertals." *Chronicle of Higher Education*, September 8, 2000, A18–A20.

———, Andrea Dorfman, and Alice Park. "What Makes Us Different?" *Time*, 2006, 44–53.

Olson, Steve. "Neanderthal Man." *Smithsonian*, October 2006, 76–82.

Schirber, Michael. "What a Tooth Reveals." *Science Now*, September 19, 2005, 3–4.

ScienceDaily. "Modern Humans, Not Neandertals, May Be Evolution's 'Odd Man Out.'" *ScienceDaily*. September. 8, 2006. http//www.sciencedaily.com/releases/2006/09 (August 2, 2007).

———."Neandertal Genome to Be Deciphered." *ScienceDaily*. July 20, 2006. http//www.sciencedaily.com/releases/2006/07 (August 2, 2007).

Scientific American. "Mapping Modernity." June 2005, 86–95.

Shipman, Pat. "Growing Up Neandertal." *American Scientist*, November 1, 2004, 506–510.

Shreeve, James. *The Neandertal Enigma: Solving the Mystery of Modern Human Origins*. New York: Avon Books, 1995.

Skomal, Susan. "Prehistory: Our Ancestors Emerge." In *World Almanac & Book of Facts*. New York: World Almanac, 2005, 503.

Smith, Fred. "The Fate of the Neandertals." *Scientific American*, April 2000, 36–37.

Sommer, Marianne. "Mirror, Mirror on the Wall: Neanderthal as Image and 'Distortion' in Early 20th-Century French Science and Press." *Social Studies of Science*, April 2006, 207–240.

Speth, John D. "News Flash: Negative Evidence Convicts Neanderthals of Gross Mental Incompetence." *World Archaeology*, December 2004, 519–526.

Spotts, Peter N. "What Happened to the Neanderthals? Check Their DNA." *Christian Science Monitor*, November 16, 2006, 1–2.

Tattersall, Ian. *The Last Neanderthal: The Rise, Success, and Mysterious Extinction of Our Closest Human Relatives.* New York: Nevraumont Publishing Company, 1999.

Tattersall, Ian, and Jeffrey H. Schwartz. *Extinct Humans.* Boulder, CO: Westview Press, 2001.

Trinkaus, Erik, and Cidalia Duarte. "The Hybrid Child from Portugal." *Scientific American*, April 2000, 32–33.

Trinkaus, Erik, and Pat Shipman. *The Neandertals: Of Skeletons, Scientists, and Scandal.* New York: Vintage, 1994.

USA Today. "Prehistory Is Not Set in Stone." November 7, 2006.

Vergano, Dan. "Scholars Debate Link between Neanderthals, *Homo sapiens.*" *USA Today*, February 9, 2005.

Wade, Nicholas. "New DNA Test Is Yielding Clues to Neanderthals." *New York Times*, November 16, 2006.

Wells, H. G. "The Grisly Folk." *Storyteller Magazine*, April 1921, http://www.trussel.com/prehist/grisly.htm (September 7, 2007).

Wilford, John Noble. "Fully Assembled at Last, Neanderthal Strides Onstage." *New York Times*, December 31, 2002, D1.

Wilson Quarterly. "The Ape That Hummed." Spring 2006, 11.

Wong, Kate. "Is Out of Africa Going Out the Door? New Doubts on a Popular Theory of Human Origins." *Scientific American*, August 1999, 13–14.

———. "The Morning of the Modern Mind." *Scientific American* Special Edition, June 2006, 74–83.

———. "Songs Without Words." *Archaeology*, March/April 2006, 54.

———. "Who Were the Neandertals?" *Scientific American*, April 2000, 98–108.

Woodard, Colin. "The Lost Tribe." *Chronicle of Higher Education*, November 19, 2004, A14–A16.

Zilhao, Joao. "Fate of the Neandertals." *Archaeology*, July/August 2000, 24–31.

Zilhao, Joao, and Francesco d'Errico. "A Case for Neandertal Culture." *Scientific American*, April 2000, 34–35.

FURTHER READING AND WEBSITES

Here are some books written for younger readers on Neandertals, human evolution, and archaeology:

Facchini, Fiorenzo. *A Day with Neanderthal Man*. Brookfield, CT: Twenty-First Century Books, 2003.

Fleisher, Paul. *Evolution*. Minneapolis: Twenty-First Century Books, 2006.

Fridell, Ron. *Decoding Life: Unraveling the Mysteries of the Genome*. Minneapolis: Twenty-First Century Books, 2005.

Lasky, Kathryn. *Traces of Life*. New York: Morrow Jr. Books, 1989.

Sloan, Christopher, Maeve Leakey, and Louise Leakey. *The Human Story: Our Evolution from Prehistoric Ancestors to Today*. Washington, DC: National Geographic Children's Books, 2004.

Tattersall, Ian, and Rob DeSalle. *Bones, Brains and DNA: The Human Genome and Human Evolution*. Piermont, NH: Bunker Hill Publishing, 2007.

Wilcox, Charlotte. *Mummies, Bones & Body Parts*. Minneapolis: Carolrhoda Books, 2000.

The meeting between early modern humans and the last Neandertals—the last time we met with another human species—has inspired fiction writers for years. These books are *kind of* about Neandertals, but they're more for fun than for facts:

Auel, Jean J. *The Clan of the Cave Bear*. New York: Bantam, 2002.

Golding, William. *The Inheritors*. New York: Harvest Books, 1963.

Gray, Luli. *Timespinners*. New York: Houghton Mifflin, 2003.

Greenburg, Dan. *Zack Files 25: Trapped in the Museum of Natural History*. New York: Grosset & Dunlap, 2002.

Scieska, Jon, and Lane Smith. *Your Mother Was a Neanderthal*. New York: Puffin, 2004.

WEBSITES

Becoming Human
http://www.becominghuman.org
> This is the interactive story of human evolution. You can listen to one of the leading Neandertal researchers, Ian Tattersall, talk about Neandertals. Click on "Launch the Documentary."

Caveman Facts
http://www.bbc.co.uk/sn/prehistoric_life/human/species/
> This BBC site offers handy facts about many hominids, including *Homo heidelbergensis, Homo neanderthalensis,* and *Homo sapiens.*

Images of Neandertals
http://www.talkorigins.org/faqs/homs/savage.html
> A gallery of artist's perceptions of Neandertals over the years is presented.

Neandertals: A Cyber Perspective by Kharlena Maria Ramanan
http://sapphire.indstate.edu/~ramanank/index.html
> The site has general information on Neandertals.

Neanderthal Museum
http://www.neanderthal.de/
> This is the official site of the Neanderthal Museum, located on the spot in the Neander Valley of Germany where the first remains were found.

Neanderthals "R" We
http://www.research.ku.edu/explore/v1n2/neander.html
> This site offers general information and a link to a gallery of Neandertal images.

VIDEO

Neanderthals on Trial. VHS. A NOVA production. Written, produced, and directed by Mark J. Davis. Boston: WGBH Educational Foundation, 2002.

ABOUT THE AUTHOR

Yvette La Pierre is the author of *Ghana in Pictures* (Visual Geography Series). She also wrote *Josephina's World*—one of the Pleasant Company American Girl books, as well as the highly acclaimed *Native American Rock Art: Messages from the Past* (Charlesbridge, 1994). She is a former editor of *National Parks* magazine and currently teaches in the Integrated Studies Program at the University of North Dakota.

PHOTO ACKNOWLEDGMENTS

The images in this book are used with permission of: © Neanderthal Museum, Germany/S. Pietrek, p. 2; © Neanderthal Museum, Germany, p. 6; © Albert J. Copley/Visuals Unlimited, p. 8; Courtesy of Marcia Ponce de León and Christoph Zollikofer, Zurich, p. 10; © Maria Stenzel/National Geographic/Getty Images, p. 11; © Laura Westlund/Independent Picture Service, pp. 13, 50, 55; © John Reader/Photo Researchers, Inc., pp. 15, 29; Library of Congress, p. 17 (LC-US262-11954); © David Gifford/Photo Researchers, Inc., p. 19; The Granger Collection, New York, p. 21; The Art Archive/Museo di Antropologia ed Etnografia Turin/Dagli Orti (A), p. 22; © Jaques Boyer/Roger-Viollet, p. 25; © Mary Evans Picture Library/The Image Works, p. 26; The Illustrated London News Picture Library, p. 27; © SPL/Photo Researchers, Inc., pp. 28, 32; © Peter Stackpole/Time & Life Pictures/Getty Images, p. 30; National Anthropological Archives, Smithsonian Institution (2007-4292), p. 34; © Richard Schlecht/National Geographic Society Image Collection, p. 35; © Gilles Tosello/Photo Researchers, Inc., pp. 37, 44; © Denis Finnin/American Museum of Natural History, p. 40; © Mission archéologique de Kébara/Photo Researchers, Inc., p. 43; © Volker Steger/Photo Researchers, Inc., pp. 46, 90; © Christina Brodie/Visuals Unlimited, p. 48; © Tom McHugh/Photo Researchers, Inc., p. 52; © Chip Clark/National Museum of Natural History, Smithsonian Institution, p. 56 (both); © Publiphoto/Photo Researchers, Inc., p. 60; © Mansell/Time & Life Pictures/Getty Images, p. 63; © Michel Grenet/Photo Researchers, Inc., p. 65; AP Photo/Joze Suhadolnik, p. 68; © Prehistoric/The Bridgeman Art Library/Getty Images, p. 70; © Volker Steger/Nordstar-"4 Million Years of Man"/Photo Researchers, Inc., p. 72; © Waltraud Grubitzsch/epa/CORBIS, p. 74; © Instituto Português de Arqueologia, p. 79; © Gianni Dagli Orti/CORBIS, p. 84; AP Photo/Jean Clottes, p. 85; © Philippe Plailly/Photo Researchers, Inc., pp. 87, 95; AP Photo/Alastair Grant, p. 92; © James King-Holmes/Photo Researchers, Inc., p. 99.

Front Cover: © Denis Finnin & Craig Chesek/American Museum of Natural History (main); © Photodisc/Getty Images (fire background).